W A T E R

AS A **SOCIAL** OPPORTUNITY

Edited by Seanna L. Davidson,
Jamie Linton,
and Warren E. Mabee

Queen's Policy Studies Series
School of Policy Studies, Queen's University
McGill-Queen's University Press
Montreal & Kingston • London • Ithaca

Queen's | Policy Studies

Publications Unit
Robert Sutherland Hall
138 Union Street
Kingston, ON, Canada
K7L 3N6
www.queensu.ca/sps/

Library and Archives Canada Cataloguing in Publication

Water as a social opportunity / edited by Seanna L. Davidson, Jamie Linton, and Warren E. Mabee.

(Queen's policy studies series)
Based on a workshop held at Queen's University in Kingston, Ontario, Canada, on November 1, 2011.
Includes bibliographical references.
Issued in print and electronic formats.
ISBN 978-1-55339-435-8 (paperback). – ISBN 978-1-55339-436-5 (epub). –
ISBN 978-1-55339-437-2 (pdf)

1. Water-supply – Social aspects – Canada. 2. Water-supply – Government policy – Canada. 3. Water quality management – Social aspects – Canada. I. Linton, Jamie, author, editor II. Mabee, Warren, editor III. Davidson, Seanna L., 1980-, author, editor IV. Series: Queen's policy studies series

HD1696.C2W28 2015   333.9100971   C2015-904127-9
                                                       C2015-904128-7

Contents

Preface

On November 1st, 2011, a workshop was held at Queen's University in Kingston, Canada, to explore the concept of *Water as a Social Opportunity*. Discussion has been ongoing since the early 2000s on the need for a domestic water strategy that meets Canada's unique needs. Key events – such as the crises associated with tainted water supplies in Walkerton, Ontario (2000) and North Battleford, Saskatchewan (2001) – were instrumental in raising the profile of water issues in the minds of the Canadian public. The ongoing plight of First Nations lacking safe drinking water on reserves across Canada remains a national shame, highlighted by continuing drinking water advisories in dozens of locations and by full-scale evacuations such as those observed in Kashechewan (2005) and Atiwapiskat (2013). The safety of our water supply – and the cost of ensuring that safety – is clearly an issue on the minds of Canadians.

Concerns about water quality have also been observed at the regional and national scale. Development of the oil sands in northern Alberta have been linked to the presence of pollutants in the region's lakes. The potential introduction or expansion of hydraulic fracturing ("fracking") operations in many provinces has led to public outcry and in some cases, calls for moratoria on future development due to fears of impacts on groundwater supply. The ongoing drought along the U.S. west coast has raised the spectre of bulk water exports and spurred discussion about the potential of climate change to increase demand on Canadian water resources.

Not all is doom and gloom. As was illustrated by participants at the Queen's workshop, responding to water challenges can bring a wide range of benefits to society. In Canada today, for example, there is growing appreciation for the opportunities that a strong water industry sector might bring. The potential for our country to learn from forward-looking policy initiatives, such as the Water Framework Directive of the European Union (2000), is recognized. Indeed, there is some impatience among a wide array of stakeholders – including industry, government, and non-governmental organizations – stemming from the fact that Canada still lacks a comprehensive strategy that might build on international examples and facilitate opportunities for both development and more effective stewardship. Some provincial action is taking place along these lines; for example, the Ontario government brought in the *Water Opportunities and Water Conservation Act* (2010), which was designed to support both conservation and the development of industrial activity around water technologies and services. At the national level, however, Canada still lacks clear policy direction.

In the pages that follow, a range of ideas around the potential of water and options for its governance are presented. The authors represent a broad selection of Canada's expertise on this topic. The editors would like to thank each of our authors for participating in the initial workshop and for bearing with us as we journeyed from the meeting to this publication. In addition, we would like to thank the Social Sciences and Humanities Research Council, which provided a Connections Grant which helped defray costs associated with the meeting, as well as the Queen's Institute for Energy and Environmental Policy and Queen's School of Policy Studies, who provided support, in both cash and human resources, to the workshop. We would like to thank the volunteers who gave much of their time to make the meeting a success: Sinead Earley, Katrina Laurant, Alice Cohen, and Geof Hall. Finally, we would like to thank Murray Clamen, Past Secretary of the Canadian Section of the International Joint Commission, for his role in the meeting, and particularly his excellent notes and comments. Finally, we would like to thank Jessica Buttery of Queen's University and Laura Cabral of Université de Sherbrooke for their work in copy-editing and preparing manuscripts for final publication.

We feel that Canada has reached a point where there is a clear gap between the expectations that our society had formed around our water resources, and the ability of our governments to develop and enact effective policy, particularly at the federal level. In a report to the Canadian Water Resources Association, Rob de Loë has suggested that a prerequisite to the development of a national water strategy is a unifying theme – a "big idea about water."[1] Recognizing the vast social opportunity associated with Canada's water resources is one such idea that might serve to drive policy development.

Warren Mabee
Kingston, 2015

---

[1] de Loë, R. 2008. Toward a Canadian National Water Strategy: Final Report. Prepared for Canadian Water Resources Association. 38pp. https://www.cwra.org/images/DocumentsLibraryAndConferenceProceedings/cnws_report_final_2008_06_18.pdf.

Water as a Social Opportunity

Jamie Linton, Ph.D.

Professor, Géolab UMR 6042 CNRS, Université de Limoges, France
Adjunct Assistant Professor, Geography and Planning, Queen's University, Canada

This book is the result of a workshop that brought people together around an idea: Rather than thinking of water as a problem, or a crisis, it is more illuminating and constructive to think of water as an opportunity. The notion of water as a social opportunity conveys the idea that the way we, as a society, respond to the water challenge has the potential to yield a wide variety of potentially positive outcomes – not just for water, or the economy but for society more broadly. In this chapter, we first introduce the concept of water as a social opportunity, describing its main theoretical and practical dimensions. Second, we summarize the three sections of the book and provide a synopsis of each chapter. Lastly, we make a pitch for considering this concept as a basis for developing a long-overdue national water strategy in Canada.

* * *

The notion of water as an economic and business opportunity has taken hold in Canada and elsewhere. As noted by Anthony Watanabe, organizer of the "Canadian Water Summit" held in Toronto in June, 2010 and a participant in our workshop, "Water has long been recognized as an important environmental issue but is only now becoming recognized as a key driver of prosperity" (quoted in Matthews 2010). This recognition of water as a driver of prosperity is at the heart of government initiatives such as Ontario's Water Opportunities and Water Conservation Act. Adopted in 2010, the main goal of this Act is to make Ontario a world leader in developing and selling technologies and services associated with the growing water conservation and treatment sector (Province of Ontario 2010). The idea of water as a business opportunity arises, in part, from growing recognition that in a world of increasing relative water scarcities and growing demands for water services, the water technology sector is on a path of exponential growth – in fact it is reported this sector is valued at more than $400 billion worldwide, and doubling every five to six years (ibid.)

As important as it may be however, the notion of water as a business opportunity reflects only a small portion of water's potential to benefit society and it is this wider idea of water as a social opportunity that the authors develop in this book. That water may be considered "a key driver of prosperity" reflects a classic theme in water scholarship. First put forward by the social theorist and historian Karl Wittfogel, the fundamental idea is that the way a society organizes itself for, and responds to hydrological challenges, has a critical bearing on the characteristics of the society itself (Wittfogel 1956, 1957). Wittfogel and others have applied this dialectical understanding of the relationship between water and society to examine historical examples where the consolidation of state power emerged as a consequence of the control and management of water on a large scale, a process that gave rise to what Wittfogel described as "hydraulic despotism." On this view, the control of water gives rise to the concentration of political power. As further argued by the American environmental historian Donald Worster, "Control over water has again and again provided an effective means of consolidating power within human groups – led, that is, to the assertion by some people of power over others" (Worster 1985).

However the basic idea of a dialectical process between water and society admits of myriad potential social and hydrological outcomes. Other examples drawn from history illustrate that the way society organizes itself to respond to the challenge(s) presented by water has yielded far more democratic forms of governance:

"For example, one of the oldest continuous western democratic institutions is the Valencia water tribunal. It operates on a rotating basis of water owners and operators resolving conflicts among other owners and operators. Variations of this system, mostly likely from Arab North Africa via medieval Spain, were actually transported to the early southwestern part of North America in the form of the aeseqia water rights systems. The Dutch water boards have operated since the Middle Ages and are widely acknowledged to have provided a model for modern Dutch democracy." (Delli Priscoli 2012, 35-36)

And contrary to the thesis of "hydraulic despotism" advanced by Wittfogel and Worster, the past few decades have witnessed a kind of paradigm shift characterized by radical changes in water governance (e.g. Gleick 1998; Bakker 2003). These changes include, among other things, a shift from emphasis on augmenting supplies of water (which usually entails the development of large-scale infrastructure) to managing demands, which involves economic and other social instruments operating at a variety of scales. Also characteristic of this paradigm shift is what might be described as the exact opposite of the classic tendency to concentrate political power. Water management in Canada and elsewhere has long since devolved from being the exclusive domain of central government authorities and now involves numerous other stakeholders at local, regional, national and international scales (de Loë 2008).

Indeed, as shown in several chapters of this volume, water provides a compelling means for engendering processes of democratic decision-making. Consistent with worldwide trends in the political economy of resources and the environment, addressing water issues raises the need for greater social participation than generally was the case in the last century. This need is reflected, in part, in the widespread discursive and structural shift from "water management" to "water governance," for which the direct engagement of broad segments of civil society is a key ingredient (de Loë and Kreutzwiser 2007; Nowlan and Bakker 2010; and see Chapter 5 by Alice Cohen in this volume). "There is no longer room for doubt – social participation in water management and governance is a reality today" (Berry and Mollard 2010, xx). As is already apparent in the trend toward more local and distributed water governance Canada (see de Loë and Kreutzwiser 2007), the imperative of public engagement in water decision-making presents an opportunity for developing new processes of democratic decision-making.

The way society responds to the host of water issues and problems we encounter therefore has the potential to yield desirable as well as undesirable outcomes – not only greater prosperity, but better forms of governance, more democratic forms of decision-making and a healthier population. Water thus represents an opportunity that extends beyond business and the economy to include the most basic questions of governance and social character. As put by Stephen Solomon in his important book on the role of water in human history: "Every era has been shaped by its response to the great water challenge of its time. And so it is unfolding – on an epic scale – today" (Solomon 2010, 4). He argues that those countries that get their act together and respond in creative ways to the growing water challenge will reap the benefits in terms of improved competitiveness, better living standards, greater social cohesion – indeed, Solomon finds great social opportunity in water.

The Organization of the Book

While Solomon makes his case in somewhat grandiose terms, the point is that the need for a response to water issues and challenges at all scales, presents opportunities for improving social relations, promoting sustainability and equity and realizing more democratic modes of governance. The idea of water as an opportunity has the potential of engaging all segments of Canadian society, all members of the water community, and all participants in the policy process. As already noted, the opportunities for business are now becoming recognized, and they will yield benefits in the right policy climate. But water presents a plethora of broader, social opportunities, many of which are described in the chapters of this book.

The book is organized in three sections: The three chapters of the first section address the broadest range of issues: They consider how responding to water problems in Canada presents opportunities for reconciling broad social goals, for developing policies based on a sound ethical footing, and for inspiring a transformative politics of decolonization across the country.

The problems of the 21ˢᵗ century are enormous and they require unprecedented ingenuity in the social capacity to respond. In this context, water may play a central role in helping realize and reconcile fundamental social objectives. In his contribution to this volume, Ralph Pentland argues that "because water is so central to human existence, meeting water challenges may very well lead the way by forcing us to reconcile the societal goals of prosperity, equity and sustainability." He begins by making the case for reconciling those goals and then argues that the water sector presents "immediate opportunities for directly harnessing market forces to the goal of sustainability, and at the same time reconciling that goal with the goals of prosperity and equity." Finally, Pentland offers seven conditions, or what he calls "water habits," that would contribute to the reconciliation of these goals.

Many Canadians (and others) have argued that realizing such goals as equity and sustainability in the water sector requires the adoption of a normative framework to guide our actions that relate to water – in other words, a water ethic (Brown and Schmidt 2010; Sandford and Phare 2011). In his contribution to this volume, Jeremy Schmidt argues that the lack of – and the need for – a water ethic in Canada presents an opportunity to develop a national water strategy and put it on a strong moral foundation. The "moral silence" of the contemporary federal public agenda, he argues, includes the water sector, "where Canada has yet to articulate a clear water ethic on which to base its water strategy." While water policies in Canada used to be based on an "object-based" communal ethic focused on "national interest," Schmidt argues that the ethical basis of Canadian water policy has since been reduced to a form of utilitarianism. "Canada's existing water ethic," he argues "is not the outworking of a rationally defended set of ethical principles." There nevertheless exists an opportunity to restore a national water ethic, based on a revised interpretation of communal interest, one that includes those (such as First Nations) who were excluded from, or harmed by, the earlier focus on a single "national interest."

The principle of equity is one of the foundation stones for developing Canadian water ethic. This might be obvious to many Canadians, given the remarkable disparity of access to safe water services in the Canadian population. For example, the deplorable condition of water services in remote First Nations' communities in Canada is well known. Rightly understood as a crisis, resolving this problem presents an opportunity for economic and cultural renewal in these communities (Linton 2010). More fundamentally, as argued by Merrell-Ann Phare and Brendan Mulligan in this volume, the many water problems faced by Indigenous peoples in Canada are giving rise to a powerful cultural and political response of "collective decolonization." Phare and Mulligan see in this process not only an opportunity to develop a transformative, ethical politics among Indigenous people in Canada, but also among non-Indigenous Canadians.

The three chapters of the second section develop the idea, already introduced above, that water presents opportunities for the development of innovative processes and structures of governance in Canada. A well-known example can be drawn from the water "crisis" occurring in Walkerton Ontario in 2000, when the town's water supply was contaminated by *E. coli*, resulting in seven deaths and over 2,300 serious illnesses. As Rob de Loë and Reid Kreutzwiser have pointed out, "The significance of the Walkerton contamination incident as a catalyst for changes in water governance in Ontario and other parts of Canada cannot be overstated" (de Loë and Kreutzwiser 2007, 94). As well as an example of how water problems present opportunities, the changes in water governance – i.e. democratic, watershed-based source protection processes – that are underway in Ontario and in other parts of Canada themselves present an opportunity for progressive modes of social organization more broadly.

In her chapter in this volume, Alice Cohen develops these ideas by considering "new and innovative opportunities to change the way we think about, act on, and govern Canadian waters." As a flow that integrates and transcends nature and society, she shows how water presents opportunities for governance processes that allow for constructive dialogue between institutions, sectors and actors that traditionally have occupied separate "silos." "Water" she argues, "presents an ideal opportunity to break down artificial distinctions between departments and jurisdictions, and it is our hope that such processes could build institutional bridges that might apply to other policy areas."

The chapter by Henning and Vibeke Bjornlund defines the key challenges for managing water in the 21st century: "Meeting new demand from existing and new consumptive users while also providing more water to the environment and dealing with the socioeconomic impact of achieving this requires radical reforms and new and innovative solutions." Developing a case study based on recent policy reforms in Alberta, they focus on two main shifts in governance processes: First, they argue that public participation in water management provides new opportunities for stakeholders and local communities. Second, they emphasize how the use of markets to reallocate water resources can provide opportunities for various social groups.

Municipalities are among the structures of governance that bear the greatest responsibilities for water management. However, municipalities in Canada are increasingly constrained by financial and political pressures to become more "cost efficient" and to reduce their control over service delivery. In her contribution to this volume, Kathryn Furlong considers municipal governance in the context of these trends. Water supply services are used as an example to explore "the opportunity to reassert the role of municipal governments in service delivery and to ask what is needed to enable municipalities to meet their wide-ranging and challenging mandates."

Water may be regarded as a social opportunity in a very basic sense – simply by virtue of the fact that water brings people together. From the countless gatherings of people at wells, springs, riverbanks and beaches throughout the ages, to the most sophisticated processes of watershed-based governance and structures of international water dispute-resolution, water is something around which people gather to talk, discuss, dispute and to make various kinds of decisions. Indeed, the capacity – or necessity – of water to draw people together is one aspect of what the anthropologist, Veronica Strang, has identified as water's essential meaning (Strang 2004 and 2005).

That water brings people together means that it presents us with myriad opportunities to cooperate. "Water," writes Aaron Wolf, "ignores all separations and boundaries save for those of the watershed itself. As such, it offers a vehicle for bringing those who share it together and, since it touches all we do and experience, it suggests a language by which we may discuss our common future" (Wolf 2012, 87). Elsewhere, Wolf, who heads the Program in Water Conflict Management and Transformation at Oregon State University, has described the process by which "[s]hared water often leads to tensions between nations, which in turn offer a vehicle for dialogue that often results in some form of joint management" (Wolf 2008, 54). This observation applies at various scales – not only between nations – such that shared water resources present challenges for which cooperation seems to be the norm. Thus, in a recent article, Jerome Delli Priscoli writes of water's powerful role in "building social community; generating wealth through provision of preconditions of economic activities; convening adversaries and providing common language for joint and creative dialogue; integrating, in a practical way, diverse interests and values; and providing a principal tool for preventive diplomacy and for building cultures of cooperation, if not peace" (Delli Priscoli 2012, 32).

These rather sanguine assessments seem to have been born out through much of Canadian experience. A classic illustration is the long record of constructive joint international management of the Great Lakes by Canada and the United States (Wolf 1998 and see Linton and Hall 2013). As shown by Rick Findlay in this volume, the Great Lakes have provided a common resource around which an innovative and influential process of discussion and issue resolution has taken shape in the form of the Great Lakes Round Table. Findlay, who was instrumental in creating the Round Table, gives an authoritative account of its emergence as an informal, collaborative, multi-stakeholder, consensus-seeking initiative. He writes passionately of its potential for revolutionizing governance in the Great Lakes basin and serving as a model for other watersheds in Canada, the U.S., and elsewhere.

The challenges of protecting smaller water bodies are equally capable of engendering exciting and innovative social responses. As Hilary Van Welter describes in her chapter, Lake Simcoe has provided the focus for a remarkable outpouring of collective, positive energy in the form of citizen actions that have sowed the seeds for a provincial protection act and a major federal funding program for the Lake. She describes two "social innovation projects" that were inspired by Lake Simcoe; a watershed initiative to restore aquatic ecosystem health known as *The Naked Truth*, and the Long Term Water Conservation Strategy developed by the Regional Municipality of York. Interestingly, in Van Welter's narrative, water's role in bringing about social change took a very active form; "water was not just as an object or a topic, but a player in the design and delivery of social innovation."

In the final chapter, Seanna Davidson tells the story of Waterlution, which involves an exploration not on the *what*, but on the *how* of innovation. Decision-making processes involving water are often characterized by classic "stakeholder"-versus-"authority" type meetings where much is discussed yet little is accomplished. While we've seen several examples of improvements in this area by municipal and provincial governments focused on source water protection and watershed based planning, Waterlution presents an example of innovative processes outside of government-based structures. In this chapter, Davidson reviews how Waterlution set out to change the way we are talking about water; to move from "siloed," sector-based, technical conversations, to cross-sectoral, inter-generational, inspired and creative facilitated dialogue.

* * *

Towards a National Water Strategy

The workshop on Water as a Social Opportunity and the publication of this book have occurred within the context of a growing interest in Canadian water policy, and especially in the development of a national (i.e. Canada-wide) strategy for water. As Thomas Axworthy, president of the Walter and Duncan Gordon Foundation put it in an op-ed piece in 2010, "water policy [is] leaping into public prominence" (Axworthy 2010). And so it has remained to the present.

Several of the reasons for this leap to prominence include:

- the general context of ever-deepening worries about freshwater issues on the global scale – i.e. the "global water crisis"

- concerns about water security occasioned by the contamination of Walkerton's drinking water supply in the spring of 2000

- growing awareness of the desperately poor drinking water quality in remote First Nations communities across the country – the most infamous example being that of Kashechewan, Ontario in 2005

- the need to address the increasing costs of water infrastructure in Canadian municipalities

- the impacts of oil sands developments on water quality and hydrological processes in northern Alberta

- concerns about the hydrological implications of climate change

- renewed concerns about international (boundary and trans-boundary) water issues with the United States

- local issues such as groundwater pollution and depletion, the growing incidence of aquatic invasive species, and contamination of surface water by agricultural runoff

- growing appreciation for the business and financial opportunities presented by developing a strong water-industry sector and by promoting greater efficiencies in water use/productivity

- the influence of forward-looking water policy initiatives in jurisdictions outside of Canada, such as the Water Framework Directive of the European Union, adopted in 2000

- impatience – on the part of water experts, NGOs, aquatic scientists, administrators, and some provincial governments – with the federal government's failure to initiate anything resembling a national water strategy

- incongruity between, on one hand, the changing interests and processes involved in making decisions about water (as reflected in the prevalence of discourses of "water governance") and on the other hand, the political and structural apparatus for making water policy, especially at the federal level. Water policy, in other words, increasingly lags behind cultural, economic and social changes that have an important bearing on water in Canada.

- a critical mass of non-governmental organizations – including professional and industry associations, charitable foundations, environmental groups, university-based research groups – with an interest in water policy

Responding to this growing interest in water, there have been several notable interventions in the water policy debate over the past several years. The common thrust of these interventions has been to call for a coordinated, national framework for water policy and governance in Canada. To cite a few examples:

- *Eau Canada: The Future of Canada's Water*, a widely-cited book edited by UBC geographer Karen Bakker and published by UBC Press was published in 2007. This book brought the question of water governance in Canada to the fore, highlighting the rather urgent need for action in updating Canadian water policy. The main significance of the book is in assembling many of the country's most authoritative voices on water into a relatively coherent argument for water policy initiatives at the national scale (Linton 2007). As Bakker points out in her concluding chapter:

  "The contrast between Canada and other jurisdictions, such as the European Union, is striking [...] Canadian water legislation is a patchwork of provincial and federal laws, and it has significant inconsistencies and gaps in responsibility and oversight. The Canadian approach to water governance has produced a set of stalemates and policy gaps. Rather than selective harmonization and subsidiarity, we have produced fragmentation and an ill-coordinated downshifting of responsibilities leaving key areas in a policy vacuum." (Bakker 2007, 365)

- In 2007, the Gordon Water Group of Concerned Scientists and Citizens published *"Changing the Flow: A Blueprint for Federal Action on Freshwater"* (Morris et al. 2007). The Gordon Water Group is an affiliation of individuals representing organizations such as the Sierra Club of Canada, the POLIS Project on Ecological Governance (at University of Victoria), the Soil and Water Conservation Society, Nature Quebec, the Program on Water Governance (at UBC), WWF Canada, and the Centre for Indigenous Environmental Resources. These groups are engaged in research projects on water issues – all of which are supported by the Walter and Duncan Gordon Foundation, which is the most noteworthy supporter of non-governmental, non-academic and non-corporate research on water issues in Canada. *Changing the Flow* offers a sustained argument for a stronger federal government role in the management, conservation and protection of water resources in Canada, as well as in promoting aquatic science: "We, like many others, recognize the need for strong federal action to help strengthen our national capacity and respond to the challenges that face us. Through our expertise and experience, we know that there is no time to waste on this critical issue" (Morris et al. 2007, ii).

- In 2008, The Canadian Water Resources Association (CWRA) commissioned Rob de Loë, to write a position paper outlining a process for developing a "Canadian National Water Strategy" (de Loë 2008). The most detailed and prescriptive initiative to date, "Toward a Canadian National Water Strategy" sets out the arguments for coordination of water policy at the national scale and suggests a detailed process by which such a strategy may be realized. Based on the recognition that "an appetite exists in organizations outside of the federal and provincial/territorial governments for national level coordination and collaboration in water management," the position paper suggests a bottom-up approach consistent with the general shift from discourses of water management to those of water governance:

"[W]ater management in Canada has long since ceased to be the exclusive domain of governments. Numerous other stakeholders – at the local, regional, national and international levels – play key roles. Thus, an inclusive, truly national water strategy will emerge only from the concerted efforts of people in organizations inside and outside of governments who believe that there is value in working together across Canada to coordinate, collaborate and share in the governing and management of water." (de Loë 2008, 9)

In 2010 The McGill Institute for the Study of Canada (MISC) hosted a national conference in April: "Canadian Water: Towards a New Strategy." The conference assembled the leading members of Canada's water community in an impressive show of support for developing a national water strategy. In her welcoming message, Antonia Maioni, Director of MISC, made the focus of the meeting clear: "Amidst growing concerns about the state of Canadian water, the goal of this conference is to promote a pan-Canadian strategy for the management of Canadian water resources" (http://www.mcgill.ca/water2010/welcome/).

In his final report to the Canadian Water Resources Association Rob de Loë identified a prerequisite to developing a national water strategy in Canada – one that has yet to be met. What is required is a unifying theme or, as he puts it, a "'big idea' about water" around which a national strategy can be shaped. He points out how such a theme has helped drive the coordination of water policy in other countries:

"[A] unifying 'big idea' about water has yet to emerge in Canada. This was a key driver in [countries that have developed coordinated water frameworks]. For example, in Australia, water reform was framed in terms of the need for micro-economic reform; in Brazil, following the 1992 Rio Conference, sustainable development became a national

                                                       Water as a Social Opportunity

priority; in the European Union, water reform was associated with the larger project of European integration. Importantly, the major ideas that drove water reform in other jurisdictions clarified the problem that would be addressed, and the benefits of pursuing an overarching strategy, policy or framework." (de Loë 2008, 23)

It was within the context of these calls for a national water strategy that the idea of a workshop on water as a social opportunity took root. The need for such a strategy in Canada was mentioned by many participants in the workshop, and is repeated in several of the contributions to this volume (but see Alice Cohen's dissenting view): For example, Ralph Pentland argues that a national water strategy can best be built "from the ground up" to focus on the needs of local citizens and managers so as to balance the goals of equity and sustainability. Jeremy Schmidt makes a well-reasoned argument for a national water strategy based on a sound ethical foundation. Merrell-Ann Phare and Brendan Mulligan argue out that "Collective decolonization will lead to the acceptance of a plurality of water ethics which will, in turn, foster stronger collaborations on water projects and clear a path to a widespread commitment to water reform, including the creation of a national water strategy."

With this volume, we wish to put forward the concept of "water as social opportunity" as a rich and compelling "big idea" to move the national water policy agenda ahead. In the meantime, the continuous challenges posed by water throughout the country are sure to present new opportunities and new possibilities for social change.

References

Axworthy, T. S. 2010. *From Walkerton to World Leaders. The Ottawa Citizen*, March 18, 2010. A13.

Bakker, K. J. 2003. *An Uncooperative Commodity: Privatizing Water in England and Wales.* Oxford, Geographical and Environmental Studies. Oxford, UK: Oxford University Press.

Bakker, K. J., ed. 2007. *Eau Canada: The Future of Canada's Water.* Vancouver and Toronto: UBC Press.

Berry, K. A., and Mollard, E., eds. 2010. *Social Participation in Water Governance and Management.* London: Earthscan.

Brown, P. G., and Schmidt, J. J., eds. 2010. *Water Ethics: Foundational Readings for Students and Professionals.* Washington/Covelo/London: Island Press.

de Loë, R. 2008. *Toward a Canadian National Water Strategy*. [Final Report prepared for the Canadian Water Resources Association]. Guelph, ON.

de Loë, R., and Kreutzwiser, R. 2007. *Challenging the Status Quo: The Evolution of Water Governance in Canada*. In "Eau Canada: The Future of Canada's Water," ed. Bakker, K. J. Vancouver and Toronto: UBC Press. 85-103.

Delli Priscoli, J. 2012. Reflections on the Nexus of Politics, Ethics, Religion and Contemporary Water Resources Decisions. *Water Policy* 14(S1): 21-40.

Gleick P. H. 1998. Water in Crisis: Paths to Sustainable Water Use. *Ecological Applications* 8(3): 571-79

Linton, J. 2007. Eau Canada: The Future of Canada's Water. *The Canadian Geographer* 51(4): 505-07.

Linton, J. 2010. *What Is Water? The History of a Modern Abstraction*. Vancouver, BC: UBC Press.

Linton J., and Hall, N. 2013. *The Great Lakes*. In "Water Without Borders: Canada, the US, and Transboundary Waters," eds. Norman, E. S., Cohen, A. and Bakker, K. J. Toronto: University of Toronto Press. 221-46.

Matthews, D. 2010. Clean 15 Series: The Water Opportunity. *Canadian Business Journal*. http://www.canadianbusinessjournal.ca/features/features_june_10/clean_15_series_the_water_opportunity.html.

Morris, T. J., Boyd, D. R., Brandes, O. M., Bruce, J. P., Hudon, M., Lucas, B., Maas, T., Nowlan, L., Pentland, R., and Phare, M. 2007. *Changing the Flow: A Blueprint for Federal Action on Freshwater*: The Gordon Water Group of Concerned Scientists and Citizens. Available from http://poliswaterproject.org/publication/127.

Nowlan, L., and Bakker, K. 2010. *Practising Shared Water Governance in Canada: A Primer*. Vancouver, BC: UBC Program on Water Governance.

Province of Ontario, Ministry of the Environment. 2010. Leading the World in Water Innovation and Conservation (Press Release). http://news.ontario.ca/ene/en/2010/05/leading-the-world-in-water-innovation-and-conservation.html.

Sandford, R. W., and Phare., M.-A. S. 2011. *Ethical Water : Learning to Value What Matters Most*. Victoria, BC: Rocky Mountain Book Ltd.

Solomon, S. 2010. *Water: The Epic Struggle for Wealth, Power, and Civilization*. New York, NY: HarperCollins Publishers.

Strang, V. 2004. *The Meaning of Water*. Oxford and New York, NY: Berg.

Strang, V. 2005. Common Senses: Water, Sensory Experience and the Generation of Meaning. *Journal of Material Culture* 10(1): 92-120.

Wittfogel, K. A. 1956. *The Hydraulic Civilizations*. In "Man's Role in Changing the Face of the Earth," ed. William L. Thomas Jr. Chicago, IL: University of Chicago Press. 152-64.

Wittfogel, K. A. 1957. *Oriental Despotism : A Comparative Study of Total Power*. New Haven, CT: Yale University Press.

Wolf, A. T. 1998. Conflict and Cooperation Along International Waterways. *Water Policy* 1(2): 251-65.

Wolf, A. T. 2008. Healing the Enlightenment Rift: Rationality, Spirituality and Shared Waters. *Journal of International Affairs* 61(2): 51-73.

Wolf, A. T. 2012. Spiritual Understandings of Conflict and Transformation and Their Contribution to Water Dialogue. *Water Policy* 14(S1): 73-88.

Worster, D. 1985. *Rivers of Empire: Water, Aridity, and the Growth of the American West*. New York, NY: Pantheon Books.

Water as an Opportunity to Reconcile Societal Goals of Prosperity, Equity and Sustainability

The Seven Water Habits of a Highly Successful Society

Ralph Pentland

President, Ralbet Enterprises, Member, Forum for Leadership on Water

We are early into the twenty-first century, and the pattern of human conflict is being fundamentally reshaped by uneven population growth and consequent migration pressures, geopolitical tensions linked to energy insecurity, widespread regional water shortages, newer forms of health-threatening contaminants, irreversible climate change and recurring global financial crises.

In fact, a recent study within the Canadian military included an entirely realistic scenario featuring a world ravaged by climate change and environmental degradation in which "markets are highly unstable" and there are high risks of widespread conflicts involving ownership and access to oil, water, food, and other resources. But, just as realistically, the way we deal with these challenges could lead to improved international cooperation and national governance, strengthened democratic decision-making and improved global security, prosperity and human health. Because water is so central to human existence, meeting the water challenges may very well lead the way by forcing us to reconcile the societal goals of prosperity, equity and sustainability (Ottawa Citizen 2011).

That reconciliation could include, for example:

- more democratic international institutions that value risk and the consequences of disproportionately allocating resources more appropriately;

- a recognition that governments, individually and collectively, have a fiduciary duty to preserve life-sustaining resources for the use and enjoyment of both present and future generations;

- an ethic which ensures that sustaining ecological services receives at least as much attention as the consumption of ecological goods;

- increased transparency, public input, and accountability in decision making;

- a significant shift towards a future that includes truly sustainable green energy and green chemistry;

- a recognition that the right kinds of regulation can actually improve innovation and the profitability and competitiveness of both industries and entire jurisdictions; and

- the strengthening and better integration of both top-down and bottom-up perspectives on and approaches to water governance.

The topic of *Water as an Opportunity to Reconcile Societal Goals of Prosperity, Equity and Sustainability* presents several interesting challenges. Those challenges will be addressed by first making the case for reconciling those societal goals, then by defining the role of water in that regard and finally by offering seven specific conditions or "water habits" that would contribute to that reconciliation of goals in much the same way as Stephen Covey did in his widely acclaimed 1989 book *The Seven Habits of Highly Effective People* (Covey 1989).

The Case for Better Reconciling Societal Goals

Societal prosperity, usually measured in terms of economic growth, is a primary goal of all governments. Equity, normally measured in terms of poverty reduction, depends upon, but does not necessarily always automatically flow from, societal prosperity. Both economic growth and current poverty reduction strategies rely upon enormous and rapidly growing flows of natural capital. Sustaining that natural capital, including our fresh water is therefore critical to meeting the goals of prosperity and equity. Conversely, sustaining our natural capital in an increasingly resource-constrained and competitive future will require a reasonably healthy and equitable national economy, creating a co-dependence between the societal goals of prosperity, equity and sustainability.

It is not difficult these days to find widely differing futures scenarios. The 2010 study by the Canadian military mentioned in the introduction is typical in that regard. At one extreme, that study envisions a scenario in which Canada would be at the forefront of a prosperous green economy, in which clean energy and environmental protection are priorities and living standards improve around the world. That best-case scenario predicts Canada taking a leadership role in the alternative energy and environmental fields, including entering into a series of technology sharing agreements and actively supporting sound international regimes and practices. At the other extreme, the study envisions a planet running out of oil and heading towards a future that could trap Canada in a violent spiral of decline in the economy and the environment. This scenario predicts a world ravaged by climate change and environmental degradation in which markets are highly unstable and there are high risks of widespread conflicts involving ownership and access to oil, water, food and other resources.

Immediately following the end of the Cold War, there was widespread optimism that we were on a path to the first scenario. It was thought that global economic growth, the promotion of democratic systems and the encouragement of international trade and investment alone would produce a virtuous cycle of wealth generation, social advances and, eventually, ecological protection. Some of that did in fact come to pass. Trade became more liberalized, some parts of the world have become more democratic and some have even become more prosperous. However, since the turn of the century, that optimism has tended to fade and many would now argue that we are presently beginning to play out the scenario where early in the twenty-first century, the virtuous cycle has morphed into a vicious cycle in which the pattern of human conflict is in fact being fundamentally reshaped by uneven population growth and consequent migration pressures, geopolitical tensions linked to energy insecurity, widespread regional water shortages, newer forms of health-threatening contaminants, irreversible climate change and recurrent global financial crises.

If we are in fact playing out this scenario, it would be helpful to consider what may have changed around the turn of the century to put us onto that path. In reality, the roots of the change likely go back a few decades earlier to the beginning of the information age and then to globalization and the global economy all of which offered enormous opportunities to spread progress equitably and in a sustainable manner all around the globe. Such opportunities were never fully realized, possibly because governments and their institutions failed to innovate fast enough to keep up with the technological revolution in the private sector.

As institutional innovation lagged further and further behind technological progress, globalization and the competitiveness agenda led to widespread deregulation, privatization and loss of some government control over many key public policy issues. As government control weakened in western style democracies, with a few notable exceptions such as the Intergovernmental Panel on Climate Change, few truly effective international governance structures filled the gap. This in turn led to insufficient overview of multi-national business decisions, a consequent under-pricing of risk and a socialization of business losses as witnessed by recurring financial crises and the public bail-out of banks and other businesses that have become ever more common around the globe in recent years (Pentland 2011).

In the environmental and water management fields, risk is underpriced by failing to internalize environmental and health costs in our systems of commerce. As a result, when society under-prices risk, it automatically creates a moral hazard that encourages ever more reckless risk-taking. In that sense, the root cause of things such as climate change, increasing chemical threats to our health and reckless energy and other resource extraction can all be quite credibly attributed to the under-pricing of environmental and health risks on a global scale. The cost of those failures will be borne by ordinary citizens for decades to come.

Fortunately, there are a lot of very talented people at least beginning to think about these things on a global scale. One such group was the Stiglitz Commission, a collection of 20 of the world's leading experts from 15 different countries. It was brought together by the United Nations General Assembly following the 2009 financial crisis. Although the Commission was advising primarily on the world's monetary and financial systems, their report also refers to interrelationships between economic and ecological issues. For example, the forward to the report notes that "the financial crisis that erupted in the United States in September 2009 is the latest and most impactful of several concurrent crises – of food, of water, of energy, and of sustainability – that are tightly interrelated." The forward goes on to point out that "our multiple crises are not the result of a failure or failures of the system. Rather, the system itself – its organization and principles, and its distorted and flawed institutional mechanisms – is the *cause* of many of these failures" (United Nations 2009). It is becoming clear that society cannot achieve real and lasting prosperity without at the same time achieving the goals of equity and sustainability.

The Role of Water in Reconciling Societal Goals

We cannot survive without biodiversity, clean air, fresh water and healthy oceans. As societies approach their regional carrying capacities, the laws of nature will eventually have to be re-elevated to at least the same level as the unnatural laws of economics. To accomplish that balancing act in a market economy the efficiencies of the free market will necessarily have to be harnessed to the goal of preserving life-sustaining and economy-supporting natural capital. For a number of reasons, some of which will be discussed below, the water sector offers some of the most immediate opportunities for directly linking market forces to the goal of sustainability and at the same time reconciling that goal with the goals of prosperity and equity.

The hydrologic cycle connects our planetary components of water, land and the atmosphere by way of a never-ending pattern of precipitation, runoff, infiltration and evaporation. As water moves continually through that hydrologic cycle it serves as the general lubricant of life, agriculture and industry. Furthermore, fresh water is arguably the most important of all the resources required for sustaining ecosystems and the services they provide to human health and well-being (UNEP 2009). Preserving water security on a global scale is clearly a lynchpin to an equitable, prosperous and sustainable future for all mankind.

Unfortunately, environmental concerns in general, and aquatic ecosystem services in particular, are often afterthoughts in economic development. Further complicating the situation is the fact that aquatic ecosystem degradation is often an incremental process with each stage of degradation going unnoticed for long periods of time. The longer-term implications for prosperity and equity are ignored until it is too late. A good example is the Aral Sea in Central Asia.

The Aral Sea used to be the third largest lake in the world. Between 1960 and 2000 its area declined by more than 60% and salinity levels tripled. All native fish species disappeared. Winds pick up millions of tons of toxic dust, poisoning nearby farmlands and contributing to respiratory illnesses. As a result, drinking water from low river flows has become hazardous and incidences of fevers and diseases are alarming. Shrinking the size of the sea has also led to a more continental climate of hotter summers and colder winters (Pentland 2004).

The short-sighted rush to immediate profit in poorly regulated global markets is more and more often leading to longer term costs to society at large that may in some cases be much larger than the immediate benefits. As observed by the Stiglitz Commission, we may have to make some very fundamental adjustments to our economic assumptions and systems in order to preserve even the world's financial systems, let alone the aquatic ecosystem services that support those systems in the long run. These adjustments will not be easy and will not happen quickly.

For example, contrary to general belief, GDP does not measure progress. It is merely a gross tally of products and services bought and sold, with no distinction between transactions that add to well-being and those that diminish it. As a measure of progress, GDP violates both basic accounting principles and common sense by treating the depletion of natural capital as income, rather than the depreciation of an asset. As a result, the more a nation depletes its natural resources by either overuse or abuse, the more the GDP increases. Equally absurd, an economic activity that creates a serious water pollution problem contributes to GDP as does the economic activity needed to clean it up which creates the illusion that pollution provides a double benefit for the economy.

Many attempts have been made to overcome deficiencies in GDP as a measure of progress. Most adjust GDP downward by removing what might be considered non-productive activities, such as fixing blunders and social decay from the past, borrowing resources from the future and the shifting of functions from the community and household realms to that of the monetized economy. Once adjusted in these ways, the indicators generally show that genuine societal progress may have peaked in the mid 1970s and has been declining ever since (Redefining Progress 1995). In many ways, repairing measures of progress and repairing water management models must necessarily go hand in hand.

The fundamental issue is that we have not yet been able to incorporate externalities related to environmental damage and impacts on human health into the way we measure progress, into our systems of commerce and into our water management decisions. In the long run, that will become absolutely necessary but it is still a long way off. In the meantime, we will have to become very ingenious at coping with and adapting to the consequences of this fundamental deficiency in the world's economic and business models, as well as its water management decisions. We are currently witnessing a lot of coping and adapting to the consequences of imperfect financial systems all around the world. We have a lesser sense of urgency with adapting to aquatic ecosystem decline due to climate change, hazardous chemicals and reckless resource extraction but there are signs of a growing sense of urgency in these areas.

Seven Conditions or "Water Habits" for Reconciling Goals

1. International Institutions that Value Risk and Apportion Losses Appropriately

As the economy globalized, we gradually adjusted some international institutions such as the World Bank, the World Trade Organization and the International Monetary Fund. But, those adjustments were far from democratic and were all focused primarily on the goal of private sector prosperity. There are no international institutions that provide sufficient oversight of multi-national business decisions and certainly no mechanisms for internalizing environmental, health care and other externalities into our systems of global commerce and water management. Until those institutional deficiencies are rectified, there is no reason to believe that we will not continue to undervalue risk and socialize costs in ways that will increase inequities, reduce sustainability and cause more and more frequent and serious economic and ecosystem dislocations.

The Stiglitz Commission report suggested that, "our global economic system must be adjusted to the requirements of an era in which the risks engendered by centuries of neglect have reached a point of extreme danger and the cost of adjustment must be borne by the present and succeeding generations." The main report further introduces a sense of urgency with statements such as, "In trying to resolve the problems of the short-run crisis, it is important to seize the opportunity to make deeper reforms that enable the world to enter the 21st century with a more equitable and stable global financial system, one which could usher in an era of enhanced prosperity for all countries."

In the water and environmental fields, the first order of business must necessarily involve much stricter application of the user and polluter pay principles.

2. Recognition of Fiduciary Duty and Public Trust

If we are to sustain the health and wellbeing of Canadians, we must necessarily recognize that certain natural resources, especially air, freshwater and oceans are central to our very existence and that governments must necessarily exercise a continuing fiduciary duty to sustain the essence of those resources for the long-term use and enjoyment of the entire population.

The notions of common property and fiduciary duty are not new ideas. In ancient Rome, air, rivers, sea and seashore were considered common property for the use of all citizens. In England, the Magna Carta of 1215 upheld the rights of ordinary citizens with respect to fishing and navigation. The French Civil Code, which perpetuated the notion of common property with respect to navigable waters and streams, was transplanted to New France, including Louisiana in the 17th Century. The Quebec Act of 1774 preserved French civil law in Canada, including notions of common property.

Public trust law has played a central role in water and environmental management in the United States since the 1970s. In Canada, public trust laws are most notable by their absence. In the United States, the public trust doctrine mirrors a historical expansion of public consciousness away from immediate private interests to the interests of society at large, future generations of citizens and even non-human life. The pervasive clash of modernity and ethical values is the very reason that we need the constancy of principles like the public trust doctrine.

If we in Canada are to achieve a sustainable future, we must eventually embrace notions at least somewhat akin to the public trust doctrine. For example, governments must "preserve and continually assure the public's ability to fully use and enjoy" common property resources. That does not mean water resources cannot be exploited in a market economy. Under the public trust doctrine as it has evolved south of the border, governments' can "recognize and convey" private proprietary interests in respect of common property but, only provided that the public interest is not "substantially" impaired (Pentland 2009).

We can reduce emerging health threats associated with newer forms of water pollution as well as preserve essential ecosystem services and we can do so in ways that will improve equity and increase our medium to long-term prosperity. This will only happen if, as our environmental laws and policies evolve, citizens demand a more binding contract with their governments that emphasizes transparency and accountability and that impose on our governments a legislated duty to preserve the life-sustaining attributes of fresh water, air, land and oceans.

3. Accounting for Ecosystem Services

One problem with relying exclusively on conventional economic theory is its failure to account for ecosystem services. Ecosystem goods refer to natural products harvested and used by humans. Ecosystem services support life by regulating essential processes such as the purification of air and water, pollination of crops, nutrient recycling, decomposition of wastes and generation and renewal of soils. The ecosystem services provided by natural systems are taken for granted because they are not formally traded and are therefore disassociated from pricing that warns of changes in supply and demand conditions. It is not only markets that fail to signal ecosystem degradation. Economic policies such as the subsidization of ecologically damaging activities frequently provide perverse incentives that actually encourage such degradation (U.K. Department of Environment, Food and Rural Affairs 2005).

In rare cases where ecosystem services are seriously considered, both the economic and environmental outcomes can benefit. For example, the watershed of the Catskill Mountains in New York used to supply water that was ranked among the best in the nation by Consumer Reports. However, once it became overwhelmed by agricultural and sewage runoff, officials began investigating the cost of an artificial filtration plant. The estimated cost was six to eight million dollars plus $300 million per year in operating expenses. Instead, they decided to invest a small fraction of that amount – $660 million in restoring the natural capital in the Catskills watershed. The funds, raised through an Environmental Bond Issue in 1997, were used to purchase land and halt development in the watershed, to compensate land owners for development restrictions on their land and to subsidize the improvement of septic systems (Ecological Society of America 2000). Clearly, we must identify and implement many more such examples.

4. Increased Transparency

If equipped with the right information, individuals can contribute directly to improved water use efficiency and the management of household wastes and pharmaceuticals. Individuals can personally avoid contact with toxic substances in a variety of ways. As consumers and as citizens, individuals can utilize their spending power in order to influence the behavior of industries and collectively demand action by their governments with respect to, for example, improved water and chemicals management and the enforcement of environmental laws. With appropriate data and information, academic and other independent policy researchers and the media can conduct more meaningful inquiries and facilitate citizen choices in constructive ways.

If they choose to do so, either governments or the non-governmental sectors can use information, communication, encouragement, peer pressure and educational strategies to convince the public of the need for change. This approach, sometimes referred to as informational regulation, relies on economic markets and public opinion as the mechanisms to bring about improved performance.

Internationally, there have been several successful experiments with informational regulation, even in circumstances where conventional regulation is weak. A good example is the introduction of a pollutant inventory in the U.S. and its consequent impact on stock prices. This approach is particularly attractive today, because technological advances are making it increasingly viable to empower citizens, communities and interconnected networks with knowledge and lobbying skills.

One particularly interesting idea that came out of a March 2010 Conference at McGill University (Slater 2010) was the concept of a water and/or environmental information agency equivalent to the Canadian Institute for Health Information (CIHI). The CIHI creates databases, carries out in-depth analyses and prepares in-depth reports to assist legislators and other stakeholders in gaining a fuller understanding of today's healthcare issues. That is exactly the kind of information that governments, independent policy researchers, the private sector, non-governmental organizations and individuals need to make informed choices regarding the equity, sustainability and profitability of our water management decisions.

5. Greener Energy and Greener Chemistry

There is an urgent need to incorporate environmental and health care costs into our systems of measurement and commerce. We are reluctant to do that because of a misplaced fear that it will inhibit our immediate prosperity. But, at some point, and we may have already reached that point, our prosperity will begin to decline if we do not appropriately account for the degradation of environmental services and the loss of natural capital. With respect to both energy and chemicals, longer-term equity, sustainability, and prosperity can only be assured by significant substitution of existing technologies with greener energy sources and greener chemistry products.

Both energy and chemicals management have important implications for water; both are serious global issues and both will ultimately require fundamental reforms. Those fundamental reforms are likely to be based on filling three gaps:

a) The data gap: Providing for the effective operation of the energy and chemicals markets by requiring that producers and their regulators generate, disclose and effectively communicate sufficient information to stakeholders regarding the hazardous properties of their processes and products;

b) The safety gap: Providing government with the legal tools necessary to identify, prioritize and take action to reduce societal hazards associated with conventional energy and synthetic chemicals; and

c) The technology gap: Building capacity related to cleaner energy and chemical usage by incorporating scientific and technical as well as legal and policy-related elements of green energy and chemistry into the world's education and research infrastructure (Lowell Center for Sustainable Production 2009).

6. Well-Designed Regulation

A very fascinating area of public policy research is the relationship between regulatory design and industrial innovation, productivity, and competitiveness. We know from the work of Michael Porter and many others who have followed him, that under the right circumstances, and with the right kind of regulatory design, stricter environmental regulations can improve industrial innovation (Porter 1991). There are also indications that, after an appropriate time lag, productivity growth rate may also be improved, especially in sectors highly exposed to outside competition (Lanoie et al. 2008). There is a pressing need for more research in this general area. The potential benefits of further defining and capitalizing on these relationships are enormous.

Most importantly, we need to sort out the reasons for conflicting research results. Why do some studies point to a positive relationship between stricter environmental regulation, productivity and competitiveness while others do not? Are they using comparable data, or are they using different types of proxy data? Have voluntary programs and mandatory disclosure systems skewed some of the research results? What exactly is the impact of time lags (Ambec et al. 2010)?

Another interesting issue relates to the relative effectiveness of market-based as opposed to technological or performance-based regulation. There is a high probability that the improved design of water pollution control regulation, especially incentive-based regulation that harnesses market forces to improved environmental outcomes, can go a very long way towards reconciling the goals of prosperity, equity and sustainability.

 Water as an Opportunity to Reconcile Societal Goals

7. Better Integration of Top-Down and Bottom-Up Perspectives

Both the new global economy and the changing face of water and environmental issues create a basic dilemma. At a local level, citizens are able to participate extensively in decisions that are becoming relatively less important, but may not be able to participate in decisions that matter a great deal. Some of the decisions that matter a great deal include the way society manages widely dispersed and potentially very hazardous chemicals, the way climate change is impacting on water resources and the impact of large-scale resource extraction on human health and the environment. At an international, national or provincial level, where these larger issues must necessarily be addressed, the opportunity for citizens to participate and influence decisions are vastly reduced. Robert Dahl once described this more general dilemma as the "paradox of democratic representation" (Dahl 1967).

Throughout the 1990s, a great deal of literature emerged about managing in an information age, much of which was aimed at addressing this paradox of democratic representation. Most of those theories suggested that the balancing of social, economic and environmental interests should take place in an integrated way at a relatively local level, which in the case of water resources would be mostly at a watershed level. Senior governments would no longer try to impose all manner of sector-specific local solutions but, they would ensure a sufficient national knowledge capacity and exercise leadership in synthesizing, interpreting and disseminating useful and appropriate information. They would also provide local entities with clear policy and regulatory frameworks that would ensure the wider interests of society were respected. In return, citizens, broadly defined, would make responsible decisions and take responsible actions.

One of the most promising approaches to strengthening and integrating top-down and bottom-up perspectives is the European Water Framework Directive. The goal of the directive is simply to improve the quality of the water environment across the EU and establish common standards and practices that safeguard its quantity and quality for the future. In 2010, Canadian researcher Émilie Lagacé did a detailed comparison of policies in the EU and Canada, conducting 40 interviews with experts on both continents and concluded that "there are tangible benefits to collaborative water governance in the EU and that comparable benefits could be achieved in Canada with a similar approach" (Lagacé 2011).

In the foreseeable future, the top-down political focus will likely continue to be on short-term prosperity, simply because election cycles are short term. But, by better integrating a bottom-up perspective, that tendency can be balanced with longer-term equity and sustainability considerations. In fact, it can be credibly argued that an optimum national water policy would be built from the ground up and focus on those things that local water managers need from senior governments to meet the needs of citizens where they live and work.

Conclusion

The prevailing view in some quarters that prosperity will automatically lead to equity and sustainability, and conversely that prosperity is even possible without equity and sustainability, is both naïve and dangerous. This is becoming obvious with widespread degradation of the world's life-sustaining aquatic ecosystems. Dealing more effectively with our water problems, which we must necessarily do to survive and thrive, will go a long way towards reconciling societal goals of prosperity, equity and sustainability.

That reconciliation will require a number of fundamental reforms beginning with more democratic international institutions, a new water ethic and recognition by all governments that they have a fiduciary duty to preserve the essence of life-sustaining natural capital for the use and enjoyment of all, including both present and future generations. More specific reforms will also be required to bring about greater transparency and accountability in decision-making, to introduce more incentive-based forms of regulation, to encourage greener energy and chemistry futures, and to explore more integrative approaches to the management of water and related resources.

These reforms will pose difficult but not insurmountable challenges. However, to meet these challenges, society will have to stop thinking of water and other forms of natural capital as mere economic entitlements and begin thinking of them as integral parts of the natural landscape that must be sustained as a perquisite to societal prosperity and equity.

References

Ambec, S., Cohen, M., Eglie, S., and Lanoie, P. 2010. The Porter Hypothesis at 20: Can Environmental Regulation Enhance Innovation and Competitiveness?, Montreal, QC (McGill University Faculty Club), June 28.

Covey, S. R. 1989. *The Seven Habits of Highly Effective People*: Free Press.

Dahl, R. A. 1967. The City in the Future of Democracy. *The American Political Science Review* 61(4): 953-70.

Ecological Society of America. 2000. *Ecosystem Services: A Primer*. American Institute of Biological Sciences, http://www.actionbioscience.org/environment/esa.html.

Lagacé, É. 2011. *Shared Water, One Framework: What Canada Can Learn from EU Water Governance*, [Water Policy Fellowship Report] Available from www.flowcanada.org/document/301.

Lanoie, P., Patry, M., and Lajeunesse, R. 2008. Environmental Regulation and Productivity: Testing the Porter Hypothesis. *Journal of Productivity Analysis* 30(2): 121-28.

Lowell Center for Sustainable Production, The Green Chemistry and Commerce Council, and The National Pollution Prevention Roundtable. 2009. *Growing the Green Economy through Green Chemistry and Design for the Environment: A Resource Guide for States and Higher Education.*: Washington State Department of Ecology.

Danger of Resource Wars "Acute." 2011. *Ottawa Citizen.*

Pentland, R. 2004. *Great Lakes Compact–Water for Sale?* In "Decision Time: Water Diversion Policy in the Great Lakes Basin," One Issue, Two Voices. Washington, D.C.: Woodrow Wilson International Center for Scholars.

Pentland, R. 2009. *Public Trust Doctrine – Potential in Canadian Water and Environmental Management.* Victoria, BC: Polis Project on Ecological Governance, University of Victoria. Available from http://poliswaterproject.org/publication/261.

Pentland, R. 2011. *Building National Water Policy from the Ground Up.* Keynote Address to the Canadian Water and Wastewater Workshop on Water Efficiency and Conservation, Ottawa, ON, October 19.

Porter, M. E. 1991. America's Green Strategy. *Scientific American* 264(4): 168.

Redefining Progress. 1995. *The Genuine Progress Indicator: Summary of Data and Methodology.* San Francisco, CA: Redefining Progress.

Scott, B. R. 2009. *The Concept of Capitalism.* Heidelberg London New York: Springer Verlag.

Slater, R. 2010. Closing comments at the McGill Institute for the Study of Canada Conference. Canadian Water: Towards A New Strategy, Montreal, QC (McGill University Faculty Club), March 26.

U.K. Department of Environment, Food and Rural Affairs. 2005. *The Economic, Social and Ecological Value of Ecosystem Services.* [Report prepared for U.K. Department of Environment, Food and Rural Affairs, January].

United Nations Environment Program (UNEP). 2009. *Water Security and Ecosystem Services: The Critical Connection.* Nairobi, Kenya : UNEP.

United Nations. 2009. *Report of the Commission of Experts of the President of the United Nations General Assembly on Reforms of the International Monetary and Financial Systems.* New York, NY.

Water
An Ethical Opportunity for Canada

Jeremy J. Schmidt

Banting Post-Doctoral Fellow, Department of Sociology and
Social Anthropology, Dalhousie University

Canadian federalism has been characterized as reticent towards its moral presuppositions. As LaSelva (1996, 171) notes, contests regarding federal-provincial divisions of power, charter rights and the role of distinct nations within Canada have tended to "either remove moral issues from the public agenda or to diminish the moral standing of one or the other of the two [provincial/federal] levels of government." This moral silence also exists in the water sector, where Canada has yet to articulate a clear water ethic on which to base its water strategy.

Does Canada have a water strategy? Yes, if we deploy the term "strategy" in the sense developed by White (1969, 9) as "a distinctive combination of aims, means and decision criteria." In this sense, Canada's water strategy has roughly followed what White (1969) described as a progression from "single purpose, single means" (i.e. dams for hydropower) to "multiple purpose, multiple means" (i.e. dams and channel maintenance for hydropower and flood control). White used this progression to draw attention to the increasingly complex factors and processes affecting water management. Canada's water strategy, however, is not the outworking of a rationally defended set of principles for dealing with increasingly complex challenges. Rather, it is the *de facto* outcome of increasingly complex water management scenarios that are set within the context of evolving notions of federalism. It is a case where the science of "muddling through" (Lindblom 1959) has resulted in a muddied policy landscape. In it, Canada's distinctive combination of aims, means and decision criteria lacks coherence.

Canada's water strategy is distinctive by virtue of contingent arrangements between various levels of government and colonial arrangements between the government and indigenous peoples, including First Nations, Inuit, and Métis. Because these inter-governmental arrangements are contingent, they are open to change. Moreover, because the honour of the Crown is at stake in meeting treaty obligations to indigenous peoples, there are strong normative reasons to rectify colonial inequities (Asch 2014). In both cases, existing water management arrangements within Canadian federalism rely on broadly held norms, or rules of right conduct, that give Canada's *de facto* strategy ethical content. This is the case because water is a limiting factor for many dimensions of human and non-human life and for livelihood projects, so the rules of conduct governing water management have the potential to incur moral goods or harms. These ethical considerations are what this chapter focuses on.

This chapter makes the case that by engaging and examining Canada's water ethic there is an opportunity to rethink Canadian water norms and Canada's strategy for addressing complex political, social, economic, and ecological demands. The chapter proceeds in three steps. First, it introduces and explains the idea of a water ethic. Second, it identifies two ethical orientations, object-given and subject-given, that provide the normative basis for Canada's (*de facto*) water strategy. These roughly map onto the trajectory from "single purpose, single means" to "multiple purposes, multiple means." Finally, it considers how both international and provincial developments in Canada may be marshaled in developing and defending a new water ethic.

Water Ethics: An Introduction

This essay uses the term "water ethic" to describe the normative principles and social customs employed to govern the human-water relationship. In previous publications (Schmidt 2010, 4) I defined a water ethic "as a normative framework guiding actions that affect water." It is clear, however, that multiple normative frameworks affect water. For instance, different values found in legal, economic, and religious norms all affect water use. In this sense, water ethics are inherently plural and concern multiple spheres of value. Some anthropologists have remarked that water is a "total social fact" because when we give it an expression we affect many spheres of spiritual, economic, and political life (Orlove and Caton 2010). For instance, a dam may provide for urban water supplies but also affect agricultural communities, recreational fishing, aesthetic appreciation, international obligations, treaty rights, wildlife migration or sites of cultural or spiritual significance.

How should we deal with the plurality of values affecting water? Two predominant ways of understanding water ethics can be identified in the literature: one philosophical, the other legal (Schmidt and Shrubsole 2013). In the philosophical view, understanding our water ethic requires identifying who or what is worthy of moral consideration and then defending those judgments with sound arguments. For instance, we might claim that all and only humans are morally relevant and then set about to defend a version of anthropocentrism. An important insight of the philosophical view is that, regardless of where the boundaries for moral consideration are drawn, they define the morally relevant community. By contrast, the legal view tempers abstract argumentation with a focus on the practical ways that social, economic, and political systems have evolved customary water norms and, in some cases, enshrined those norms in formal laws. In this view there may be multiple types of actors (i.e. men, women or non-humans) that participate in various social or economic systems that affect water. An important insight of the legal view is that different spheres of value found in law can affect water norms, such as when national laws regarding public fishing or navigation rights come into conflict with provincial laws of resource ownership or with First Nations rights. A legal orientation towards water ethics highlights how different spheres of value implicate different scales at which political communities articulate, defend, or avail themselves of norms (see generally, Mason 2000). For instance, if a municipal or provincial law allows for certain types of activities that cause harm, individuals or communities may avail themselves of national laws, or those protecting international human rights, depending on the nature of the problem. This is important because when the spheres of value at one scale are unjust there may be other laws, replete with the values that support them, that can be used to address inequity.

The moral community identified by philosophical approaches is not always synonymous with the political community of legal approaches. This is because some of those to whom moral consideration is due may not be part of a practical governance system. For example, we may all agree that children deserve moral consideration yet differ about what age and circumstances enable them to be active participants in a political community, such as in voting or participating in water use decisions. Conversely, traditionally oppressed groups, such as women or First Nations, Inuit and Métis people in Canada, may not be included in the political decisions affecting water that they have a right to be a part of (see Gaard 2001; Phare 2009; Desbiens 2013). The view taken here is that water ethics fit between philosophical arguments and the social and political contexts that affect practical governance systems (i.e. law and policy). The aim of examining water ethics, then, is to introduce new ideas and values, to defend them with reasons, and to do so in the context of prevailing norms (see also Schmidt and Peppard 2014).

There are two reasons to consider water ethics from a perspective that looks at new ideas and values as well as practical governance systems. First, values can and do change over time in response to environmental, economic, technological, and cultural shifts (Dietz et al. 2005). Second, humans have a dynamic and co-evolving relationship with the world. As such, it is important to consider how previous ways of interacting with water have shaped complex social and ecological systems (Delli Priscoli 2000; Folke 2003). In Canada, this includes rejecting both the assumption that prior to European settlement the landscape was empty – *terra nullius* – and the assumption that no sovereign claims to its land and waters existed (Simpson 2014; Coulthard 2014). Together, philosophical and practical assessments offer the opportunity to take a values-based approach to the inherited values, competing alternatives, and alternate ways of ordering water in both material and moral terms (Groenfeldt and Schmidt 2013).

One final distinction is in order. It relates to how we reason about ethics. The following discussion sets out two different ways of reasoning about ethics from Derek Parfit (2011). The first is an "object-given" view where our reasons "are provided by the facts that make certain outcomes worth producing or preventing, or make certain things worth doing for their own sake." The alternate is a "subject-given" view where our reasons are provided by the preferences or desires that affect our actions under certain conditions. That is, in subject-given approaches our reasons depend on facts about us. In this essay, the difference between these two styles of reasoning is used to contrast ethical claims that rely on facts about the water community (object-given) versus those driven by the preferences of individuals (subject-given). Drawing this distinction also has a secondary purpose, which is to avoid prescribing an answer regarding what ethic we ought to pursue. The argument advanced below depends on facts about the water community itself. Determining those facts pitches the argument of this essay back into the political considerations of water strategies and Canadian federalism, but this time in an explicitly ethical mindset as opposed to moral silence.

Canada's Water Ethic

Does Canada have a water ethic? Yes it does. If we were to characterize that ethic relative to Canadian resource policy generally, we might say it emphasizes resource extraction, elite decision making by industry and government, and a utilitarian philosophy supporting capitalist forms of economic growth (Hessing et al. 2005). However, if we were to give a more nuanced account, we might begin from the premise that Canada's laws and policies overlay both philosophical principles and practical governance systems onto the landscapes that support cities, rural communities, and the economy. Unfortunately, Canada's water ethic has not been clearly articulated. Instead, it has been shaped by environmental and cultural factors, such as water scarcity in western Canada, and the colonization of indigenous peoples. There are too many water ethics to detail closely in as large and diverse a country as Canada, so here I take a different tack and offer an assessment of two orientations to water management in Canada. The first is characterized by narrow policy ends, the "single purpose, single means" strategies mentioned above. The subsequent period is one in which water demands multiply alongside the growing, pluralistic demands of Canadian society. Examining the ethical orientations of these two periods reveals corollary shifts between object-given versus subject-given ways of providing normative reasons for different water policies.

Object-Given Water Ethics

Object-given reasons for Canadian water policy are the historical norm. Objects are "all events in the sense that includes acts, processes, and states of affairs" and about which there may be a wide ranging set of political contests (Parfit 2011, 43). In Canada, however, these events are all structured by an on-going colonial project through which First Nations are excluded from obtaining formal water rights in Canada (see Phare 2009). This exclusion worked in favor of achieving other ends, such as enhancing the "national interest." This section surveys how Canadian water policy rationale derives from a singular object that construes the political community through a "national" lens and then embeds a natural assumption that the moral community overlaps with, or may even be synonymous with, the political community. It then considers how that assumption was challenged in the evolution from "single-purpose, single-means" to more complex and multiple water demands. Dealing with this multiplicity catalyzed the shift to subject-given ethics in Canada's water policy rationale.

Controlling water has been a central and often defining feature of modern nation states (Blackbourn 2006; Solomon 2010). In North America, securing water in the national interest was most forcefully articulated by the architect Conservation Era policies in the United States at the turn of the 20th century. At that time, WJ McGee (1911) argued for a utilitarian ethic that would manage water "in the public interest for the greatest good, to the greatest number, for the longest time." This ethic builds on the political liberalism of John Stuart Mill. Mill's combination of utilitarianism and political liberalism, however, was not all that McGee adopted. He also installed the ethnocentric assumption that the government reflected the will of "the People" and that Americans were more advanced than indigenous peoples (Schmidt 2014a). In this view, not only were state institutions properly accorded stewardship of natural resources, the management of water resources should enhance the prospects of liberal society in America. Another reason for state resource management and for managing water in the "public interest" was that the *laissez-faire* resource economics of private enterprise was leading to massive deforestation and agricultural erosion on the American frontier (Merchant 1997). In Canada, similar trends were evident. Here, water development was also initially linked to private enterprise for trade and commerce, and in small-scale hydropower development, but later came to be dominated by state-run exercises (see Creighton 2002; Nelles 2005; Manore 2006; Armstrong et al. 2009).

Canada also pursued a utilitarian ethic in support of liberal society. It began by claiming that the total utility derived from private water projects was less than could be achieved under large-scale developments. As such, the "public interest" was not always maximized through private development because the large costs associated with developing water resources were too high for individual firms. In this regard, a sentiment grew that developing water reflected a kind of duty that the Canadian public owed to itself and which the government was charged with expressing. For instance, as Canada opened the west to settlement, the architect of the 1894 *North-west Irrigation Act,* William Pearce (1891), argued in a letter to the Minister of the Interior, William Burgess, that "[w]ater in a country dependent on irrigation is so precious that it is a duty the Government owes to the community, or, in other words, that the community owes to itself, to prevent its being captured by monopolists and sold to the farmers, who must buy it at any cost, at extortionate prices." In Pearce's (1891) view, private development of water would result in only partial development or "in other words, a considerable loss of national wealth." And so, when the *North-west Irrigation Act* became law across present day Alberta, Saskatchewan and Manitoba, the government took the lead in water development financing, water ownership, and in decisions about water allocation.

The vision articulated by William Pearce saw the government as reflecting both moral and political duties that "the community owes to itself." Pearce's language recalls that of another Canadian, Charles Taylor (2004), who argued that appeals to a "community" that comes together to legitimate the constitutional state is a distinctively modern way of imagining social life and of conceiving of the common ways that material and moral orders gain legitimacy. It is in this way that developing water for the "national interest" came to be seen as a duty that the political community "owes to itself" in a moral sense. In short, aligning the material order of water with the moral order of the community became the objective of water policy. Further, in this formulation the "public interest" coincided neatly with the "national interest." This is perhaps not surprising given that the 1894 *North-west Irrigation Act* was explicitly designed to facilitate western settlement, which was a key national objective in the late 19th century.

The object-given rationale provided by the coincidence of the national interest and that of the "community" was not unique to western Canada. It was reflected in other Canadian laws as well. Quebec's civil code, for instance, follows the doctrine of *res nullius* wherein water is not the kind of thing that can be owned (Cantin Cumyn 2007). Rather, water belongs to the community. As Glenn (2010, 501) argues, even though there is no counterpart to *res nullius* in the common law

                                   Water: An Ethical Opportunity for Canada

traditions of Canada outside Quebec, there is a residual notion that the government is a steward of water and that, because of water's foundational importance to life, "it is inconceivable that Crown ownership of water *in situ* [literally: in place] is full and absolute, giving the Crown the right to do with the water whatever it wants." When the federal government divested authority and ownership of resources to the provinces, norms that limit water policy to that which is good for the community were carried over. The roots of many provincial water doctrines that establish rights to water in Canada, such as the prior appropriation (first-in-time, first-in-right) laws that prevail on the prairies or the riparian laws more common in the east, are built on recognition that water is a communal good and that the political community has moral obligations to steward it as such (Schorr 2005; Hanemann 2006). As legal expert Joseph Sax (1994, 35) put it, norms that tie water to place "…keep [water] within the community as a community resource."

In Canada, and for a great deal of the 20th century, the state was seen as the primary actor in securing water to meet moral obligations to the political community. The fulfillment of these obligations was achieved largely by increasing water supply (Sprague 2007). Many regions and sectors prospered under the model of increasing the supply of water for sanitation, drinking water, hydropower, industry, and agriculture. But there have been, and continue to be, stark and reverberating failures regarding who and what has been excluded from the benefits, or borne the costs, of water supply developments (see Phare 2009; Benidickson 2007; Parr 2010). These shortcomings are not only the outcomes of unforeseen effects of development, they are also the effect of political claims regarding *which* political community water policies should serve and deriving object-given rationale from *those* ends. For instance, the denial of First Nations water rights is prevalent across Canada, yet the communal ends that justify such oppression vary; Quebec nationalism was asserted through identity-forming hydroelectric development in the 1970s yet simultaneously denied the sovereign claims of the James Bay Cree (Desbiens 2013).

While the idea that water policy rationale derives from a singular political community is the historical norm, it has not gone unchallenged. Furthermore, it has been challenged in particular ways. As Desbiens (2004, 2007, 2013) has shown, First Nations challenges to Quebec's James Bay hydroelectric projects took aim at both the sentiments and symbols of Quebec nationalism and the colonial projects of European settlement. Ultimately, the efforts of the James Bay Cree helped usher in a new era of settling land claims in Canada (see Asch 2014). A second way that singular policy rationales have been questioned is through the local, lived experiences of those affected by water development. Many individuals and communities have been marginalized through large hydropower projects increased welfare through aggregate measures of utility but nevertheless had significant negative effects (see Parr 2010). Subsequently, these individuals often formed coalitions to advocate for their health and livelihoods. These coalitions have at times combined with a third, scientific avenue of questioning. This perspective focuses on the negative outcomes of supply-side water management and its failure to respect to ecological context. These coalitions and scientific lines of questioning found common-cause during the large protests, legal challenges, and opposition to Alberta's Oldman Dam in the 1980s (see Glenn 1999). Those protests, and legal victories, gave rise to a significant change in water policy in Alberta (Heinmiller 2013). It was a change in policy rationale that, as the next section considers, mirrored broader shifts from object-given to subject-given norms more broadly.

Before moving to the next section, it is worth highlighting that challenges to the idea that water policy rationale derives from a singular object, a nationally unified "public interest" also work to undermine the assumption that the moral community overlaps with the political community. Recall that the broader arguments for this assumption are built on both utilitarian ethics and political liberalism. This, historically, has been the approach to water policy taken within Canadian federalism. When this idea reached it limits it did so in tandem with recognition that water management strategies must accommodate multiple purposes and multiple means. Neither of these necessarily requires departing from utilitarianism or political liberalism. For instance, because utilitarianism does not stipulate how to achieve the greatest good, multiple avenues are available so long as they produce the best outcomes. Likewise, liberalism allows individuals to freely pursue their life projects provided that they do not harm others and that they do not harm themselves irreparably (Barkley and Seckler 1972). In principle, the limits of supply-side water management could have led to a careful re-evaluation of the assumptions about the political and moral community that water policy in Canada was oriented towards. But it did not. Rather, forms of liberal, utilitarian water management continued through subject-given rationale for water policy.

Subject-Given Water Ethics

Several authors have argued that over the course of the 20th century resource management generally shifted from "bureaucratic utilitarianism" to "individualist utilitarianism" as the role of government gradually shifted from direct management to one of "setting the rules" (Norton 2005; Brown 2008). Setting the rules typically came through a combination of individualistic models that focused on economic tools and private market transactions for resource governance or by models built on stakeholder representation and participatory decision making (see Durant et al. 2004; Sabatier et al. 2005). Importantly, these new models retained the same water ethic (Feldman 1995). What is different is the rationale behind government policies. The rationale for past policies was the "national interest" and the goods provided for by ensuring water for the community. The rationale for contemporary policies, by contrast, comes from facts about the preferences of individuals. This is the shift from object-given to subject-given reasoning.

In Canada, the start of the shift towards subject-given policy rationale is not easy to pinpoint, but there have been some distinct signals. The first was the sharp questioning of the so-called "myth of abundance" (see Sprague 2007). This questioning targeted the assumption that water supply could increase indefinitely. Increases in supply met utilitarian demands only if the goods derived from more water outweighed the harms that came along with increased supply. This also challenged liberal solutions that relied on allocating new supplies of water as part of dealing with conflicts. As previously discussed, different notions of the good increasingly challenged this model both because it required First Nations articulate their claims in ways that liberal states would recognize (rather than on their own terms) and because it did not adequately take ecological considerations into account. Yet Canada's water ethic did not change. Rather, a new defense for it was offered, one that shifted to subject-given reasons. To characterize this shift, it is helpful to position it within the broader discourses that were then at work in Canadian federalism. One such marker came in the 1985 Royal Commission on the Economic Union and Development Prospects for Canada. The commission reported that,

"The task of governments is to meet the preferences of citizens who happen to be in the provinces or in the country they have been elected to govern. Meaningful provincial communities do not exist, except as provinces." (Breton 1985, 505, original emphasis)

This statement from the Royal Commission was interpreted in 1992 by Kennett (1992, 10) to argue that, in Canada, "... conceptions of community appear to have limited relevance to the design of federalism as it relates to water management." But, given the evidence presented above, Kennett's claim is incorrect. Something else is afoot, and that is the denial that communities exist at all. At first glance the Royal Commission's declaration that communities do not exist, except as provinces, appears perplexing. It can be read as implying that there is no *particular* community that governments should serve. Rather, governments serve the aggregate of individuals. As such, individual preferences provide the facts from which to derive policy rationale. This is a subject-given approach, the implications of which are highly varied across Canada. In general, however, there has been a trend away from federal involvement in favor of provincial and/or regional autonomy in the serving of individual preferences. The cap-stone of this period may perhaps be the legislative changes in 2012 to both the *Fisheries Act* and what was formerly known as the *Navigable Waters Protection Act*. The changes to these laws significantly reduced federal oversight of water in Canada.

The reorientation of water policy rationale from what is good for the "national interest" to the satisfaction of individual preferences represents a critical ethical change. This is because when the recognition of multiple, complex challenges to Canada's water development path arose, the shift to subject-given policy rationale was a choice against revisiting or expanding the notion of "community" that had previously served to provide object-given rationale for water policies. As a result, the turn to subject-given policy rationale continues to extend, albeit in a new guise, the utilitarian, liberal norms of Canadian water policy. The upshot is that many historical inequities persist, particularly the colonial structure that requires sovereign indigenous claims to be reconciled to the state. Further, in this new iteration the substantive considerations of what is good for the community are replaced with procedural considerations that operate with respect to individual preferences. In short, policies are not oriented to *any* community but are instead oriented to the aggregate interests of individuals.

Creating policies based on individual preferences requires methods for determining what those preferences are. This has been accomplished using two techniques. First, there has been an increased emphasis on the role of economics. For instance, a water market for transferring allocation licenses in Southern Alberta was created in 2002 (Alberta Environment 2002). The market works on the principle that willing buyers and sellers are best able to determine the highest value to which water should be put. Alberta's market model assumes that transactions reveal the preferences of individuals involved in them (Schmidt 2011). There are several reasons why that assumption fails. One is that transactions only reveal that a transaction took place. They say little, if anything, about *why* it took place and hence reveal little if anything about individual preferences (see Sagoff 2004). A more nuanced approach has characterized the re-regulation of municipal water services. In Ontario for instance, policies now allow for the private management of operations, corporate service provision, and other forms of delegated management (see Bakker and Cameron 2005). However, even these formats have drawbacks because the shift towards subject-given policy rationale does not address the inequities produced by earlier policies. In southern Ontario, for instance, the restructuring of urban water utilities has led to efficiencies for some larger centers while creating increased burdens on downstream water users, such as First Nations. Mascarenhas (2012) offers an example of this in London, Ontario where a new wastewater treatment plant, with a capacity of 4 million gallons per day, was constructed just three kilometers upstream of the Oneida First Nations despite their requests for a full provincial environmental assessment before a decision was reached.

A second technique for determining individual preferences is to develop mechanisms and institutions for stakeholder participation. Frequently, these new institutions have used the river-basin, or watershed, as the spatial scale for water management decisions. Efforts in watershed management have been strikingly diverse across Canada (see Senecal and Madramootoo 2005). Ontario's water conservation authorities, for example, were formed between 1946 and 1979 and have had to evolve as different governments alter funding arrangements and as new challenges, such as protecting municipal water sources, became increasingly important tasks (Mitchell et al. 2014). Elsewhere in Canada, however, new water management arrangements did not always have the same legal mandate as Ontario's conservation authorities. Often, the explanations offered for new arrangements varied while what ambiguity arose regarding what the aims of watershed management were because different stakeholders took up ideas and concepts in different ways (Cohen 2012). From a policy perspective, the rationale for stakeholder participation is to generate consensus through procedures that include participation of those affected by decisions. This is offered as an alternate route to establishing legitimacy (see Sabatier et al. 2005).

There are several ethical difficulties with determining ethical legitimacy through participatory governance. First, making decisions via procedural mechanisms requires that all values are commensurate. This requirement is often not met because different cultural groups often hold different kinds of values (Espelund 1998). As such, there remains a role for the Canadian government beyond "setting the rules" because reconciling different substantive goods, such as those of First Nations, incurs federal obligations (see also Weibust 2009). Second, not all of those affected by water policy decisions are correctly categorized as stakeholders. Future generations, for example, are not correctly classified as stakeholders yet they will be affected by policy decisions (see Kysar 2010). Third, the rules governing how stakeholders participate in decisions can only be fair if there is consent on those rules. For instance, First Nations have unique constitutional standing through both historic treaties and modern land-claim agreements and so the design and practice of political participation should reflect and respect this (see Tully 1995).

Despite the turn to subject-given policy rationale, communities still matter. Because of this, Canada's turn to subject-given water ethics faces a two-fold problem. It begins without rectifying historical injustices. In this sense, rather than considering *which* community previous water policies served and then seeking appropriate remedies for those who did not benefit or were harmed by policies serving the "national interest," the direction chosen was to deny that *any* communities existed. Second, subject-given water ethics promote procedural techniques for determining individual preferences over the substantive concerns of different communities or alternate procedures for reaching agreement. In addition, subject-given policies run into an even more basic problem because they deny the fact that the decision to pursue subject-given rationale was undertaken by a particular *political community* (Kysar 2010). This is a serious ethical difficulty, since it is increasingly recognized that social relationships to water are produced through the specific ways that we interact with, share, and govern water (Orlove and Caton 2010). As such, the attempt to govern water without reference to those specific relationships places additional burden on procedural forums that must answer questions that involve different philosophical and legal conceptions of what is good (Tisdell 2003). The next section of this essay suggests that the turn to subject-given rationale should be reconsidered.

Toward a New Water Ethic

In this essay I have been following Parfit's (2011) distinction between object-given and subject-given ethics. For philosophical reasons I believe the former is superior. For practical reasons I believe that the use of an object-given ethic would be prudent for Canadian water policy. It is philosophically superior because it allows reasons for water ethics that are based on objects that are deemed good in themselves and from this it follows that policies could allow for different substantive conceptions of what is good. This leads to the following questions. What are those objects? Which communities do they issue from and, in turn, support? And what practical reasons are there for Canadian policy to work towards respecting these different communities and the objects they hold as intrinsically good? The concluding section will respond to these questions by considering the international dimension of Canadian water policy and the recent developments of provincial water strategies. These strategies are not the *de facto* outcomes of federalism. Rather, in response to existing arrangements they are explicit attempts to fashion and execute a particular set of aims, means, and decision criteria in accordance with new or alternate values. Some provinces, such as Alberta, have explicitly described their water strategies as creating the possibility for a new water ethic (Alberta Water Council 2007).

What objects can serve as intrinsically good ends for water policy? As this essay has argued, the initial object-given rationale for Canada's *de facto* water strategy was the "national interest" as construed through different appeals (recall the unique Quebec case) to the community that gave democratic legitimacy to the state. In Canada, this definition of "community" had its most marked effect in excluding the legitimate claims of, and agreements with, indigenous First Nations, Inuit and Métis. Where these claims were recognized they were subordinated to the sovereignty of the Crown (Phare 2009). Rather than engage in substantive debate regarding exclusion, the turn to subject-given ethics denied that any communities existed. This is not to say that communities suddenly vanished or that local-level decisions are not still made with a particular group in mind. These politics are certainly still in play. Rather, it is to note that the turn to subject-given policy rationale in Canadian federalism sought legitimacy without reference to any particular community. Instead of opening ideas of "community" to include the realities of agreements with First Nations or Canada's ecological context, policies were oriented to the preferences of individuals. Trends towards decentralized decision making and experiments with water markets within Canada, however, have one significant exception. Namely, Canada retains an object-given policy position in international water policy.

Canada retains an object-given approach to policy rationale through the International Joint Commission (IJC), which is comprised of representatives from the United States and Canada to manage transboundary waters. The IJC operates in reference to a 1909 treaty between two nations and their competing "national interests." The terms recall a time when the moral and political communities affected by water were largely understood to overlap. More recently, the IJC (2009) has sought to incorporate an "ecosystem approach" that would see transboundary agreements formed and enacted in the best interest of not just watercourses themselves, such as rivers or lakes, but of the entire ecosystems that are responsible for healthy watercourses. This approach represents an alternate basis for object-given policy rationale. It is one premised on respect for the different ends that each nation may hold and which views those ends as premised upon healthy aquatic ecosystems. In this sense, the good of healthy ecosystems operates as an intrinsic end for both Canadian and American transboundary water management.

The "ecosystem approach" taken by the IJC does not depart from utilitarianism. And, in an interesting way, it also does not conflict with the subject-given ethics that characterize domestic water policy in Canada. It walks this fine line by drawing a distinction between the object-given basis of normative legitimacy provided for by healthy ecosystems and the use of a subject-given form of valuing those ecosystems. This is evident in the IJC's (2009) appeal to the economic valuation of "ecosystem services," which is a form of economic valuation that seeks to value natural processes in terms of what it would cost to produce comparable benefits through alternate means. For instance, ecosystem services valuation may estimate how much we would pay for purifying water using water treatment plants if wetlands that presently perform this function were removed for urban development. Problematically, this requires the use of only those ecological models that fit with economic ones even if those ecological models provide only partial pictures of complex systems (see Norgaard 2010). It is a subtle, although important, distinction because how we value ecosystem services depends on our preferences and not on the total scientific resources we have for determining the goods of healthy ecosystems. Wetlands, for instance, provide for many more goods than just clean water, such as flood protection and habitat for resident and migratory species. As such, valuing ecosystem services is not a straightforward or necessarily sufficient path. It may be a start, however, and will be discussed further in the conclusion of this essay.

Why is it prudent to work towards a new water ethic based on object-given policy rationale? One reason is to counter the shift to subject-given policy rationale in Canada, which has been premised on two false assumptions. The first assumption is that communities do not exist or, in weaker form, that public policy should not be justified in relation to any particular community. This premise is logically unsound because the decision to deploy subject-given policy rationale is one that is made by a specific political community (see Kysar 2010). The second assumption is that satisfying individual preferences will, in sum, produce the most benefit to all. This premise fails because the uneven and unequal conditions created by previous policies remain unaddressed, particularly those affecting First Nations but also those affecting ecosystems. Interestingly, and despite the introduction of subject-given rationale for water policy and management, several provinces have recently devised new water strategies to search for substantive solutions to water challenges.

The Nova Scotia (2010) water strategy, Alberta's water strategy (2003) and Quebec's national water policy (2002) each promote water stewardship as an object-given end. That is, water stewardship is seen as intrinsically good, an end in itself. As one might expect, the object-given rationale for these policies is constrained to its own jurisdiction. Again, and in similar fashion to the IJC example above, within these jurisdictions there is an awkward attempt to combine subject-given valuation methods with object-given rationale. For instance, the Northwest Territory's (2010, 71) strategy is explicit in its consideration of both economic and non-economic values in water planning:

"Economic measures form only one reference point for making decisions. Many of the values held by NWT residents regarding water cannot be measured in economic terms […] When these values are expressed in economic terms, there is often no consensus on the value attributed to a specific interest or use."

                                              Water: An Ethical Opportunity for Canada

Part of the reason that there is no consensus on the values "attributed to a specific interest or use" is that not all values are commensurable and, consequently, not all policy ends are compatible. This means that substantive differences are likely to remain even *after* individual preferences are (theoretically) known. In this sense, even though emerging water strategies amongst Canadian provinces and territories are oriented towards the public good of water stewardship there is often no consensus on what that means. Rather, the aim of shared governance practices is to see how the good of "water stewardship" may come about through procedural mechanisms. These new forums for participation, however, are not laid on an even context. For instance, small rural municipalities and independent landowners (i.e. farmers) may not have the capacity to participate in shared governance procedures that require significant travel for meetings where decisions are made. In addition, the colonial context in which procedural governance techniques are formulated and implemented is often unfit for Canada's federalist context because it continues the denial of alternate goods unless they conform to the notion of "stewardship" allowed for by new water strategies. Depending on the terms of participation, indigenous groups may wish to abstain from provincial-level exercises. In some cases, such as in Alberta, provincial water strategies enable participation but provide only informal inputs into regulations and this means there is no guarantee that procedural exercises will ultimately affect decisions (Schmidt 2014b).

The IJC and provincial water strategies both reflect the tensions between object-given and subject-given water ethics. In part, this tension exists because of broader discursive turns towards subject-given policy rationale in Canadian federalism. It is within this tension that opportunities for new ethical opportunities may be found. With a closer consideration of the disposition to object-given ethics in what I introduced initially as a *de facto* water strategy in hand, there is a historical context to position the more recent development in water policies at the federal, provincial and international level within: Canada's water ethos began with a sense that the government sought the moral good of a political community. In this sense it was decidedly singular. As water demands multiplied, the notion of "community" was challenged by those who imagined new moral and material orders for water based on rectifying colonial inequities and linking water policy more carefully to ecological context. In its place, recent decades have witnessed a shift towards subject-given approaches to water ethics in Canada, some of which were reviewed above. These approaches are premised on the idea that the preferences of individuals can be managed through procedural mechanisms, such as those offered by economics or forms of shared governance. Yet this turn is itself the decision of a particular political community. As such, the decision to employ subject-given policy rationale did not make room for different *kinds* of goods that may be held by indigenous peoples, or for the goods provided for by different *kinds* of objects held as intrinsically good, such as healthy aquatic ecosystems.

Conclusion: Opportunities for Water Ethics in Canada

Canada's existing water ethic is not the outworking of a rationally defended set of ethical principles. This chapter highlighted how Canada's initial, object-given water ethic was challenged by those who were excluded from, or harmed by, its focus on a single "national interest." I argued that the turn to subject-given ethics tried to circumvent the problem of *which* "community" benefited from the default water strategy that had evolved in Canadian federalism. I also argued that subject-given policy rationale has significant shortcomings in terms of its reliance on economics and shared governance methods that are based on determinations of individual preferences. I outlined several difficulties with these methods, and their shared failure to acknowledge that the decision to pursue subject-given policies was made by a particular community. Attempts to define alternate objects for policy rationale, either in ecosystem approaches or provincial water strategies, are now entangled with the turn towards subject-given policy rationale in Canada. The fit between the two is uneasy, but provides an opportunity to rethink Canada's water strategy alongside the increasingly complex demands being made on water.

Demands on Canada's water systems are complex. As Sandford and Phare (2011) point out, they are not only socially complex, they also operate within a hydrological cycle that is in constant flux as it responds to human activities (see also Milly et al. 2008). Kay (2000) masterfully argued that our uncertainty with respect to complex systems necessitates that we acknowledge how our perspective is neither unbiased nor complete. Our perspective is always positioned and partial. Because of this, linking science to policy never value free. Rather, different policy options reflect our own positions and values (Ioris 2012). Once this is recognized it can be best addressed not by arguing that there are no particular communities for policy rationale but by arguing that there are multiple communities from which we can derive sound normative reasons regarding the aims, means, and criteria of water management. These different communities all depend on the goods that healthy ecosystems provide. Canada retains the capacity to organize water policy in line with the goods provided for by healthy ecosystems, as the example from the International Joint Commission provided. This means that, in principle, Canada's water strategy is open to being reorganized accordingly and with explicit attention to the values that link science to policy.

                                        Water: An Ethical Opportunity for Canada

The notion of "water stewardship" in many provincial water strategies attempts to provide a shared imagining of healthy water systems even though there are complex realities of achieving water stewardship for urban, rural, and aquatic communities (see Annear et al. 2002). As such, the concept of water stewardship could offer a bridge from existing practices to new water ethics if it is understood as part of supporting a variety of different goods. For instance, water stewardship cannot be achieved solely through the valuation of ecosystem services because this would not adequately account for the scientific and cultural values that do not conform to economics.

Finally, Canada's water ethic is the outcome of its *de facto* water strategy. This strategy began by privileging the "national interest" and has not yet come to terms with the substantive moral failings of that decision. A change in Canada's water ethic must include a clear and consistent place for the sovereign claims of indigenous First Nations, Inuit and Métis. This change will require decisions by the one political community currently benefiting from federal arrangements to include multiple communities. In many cases the template offered by meeting treaty obligations to indigenous peoples is the obvious and important step. Where no agreements are in place, negotiations are needed. The current turn toward subject-given approaches to water management has significant shortcomings but changes are both possible and feasible. Here, Canada must recover its historical disposition towards object-given policy rationale in the context of revisiting the constitution of the moral and political communities that "owes to itself" the duty of sound water policy. We must identify the intrinsic ends towards which water policy should be oriented in a manner that supports multiple goods across different social and ecological communities. It is against the spirit of this paper to define those goods *a priori* as this might preclude opportunities that only arise through fair and open democratic practices. It is through such practices that the door may be opened to retooling the aims, means, and decision criteria that are required to create an ethically sound water strategy for Canada.

Acknowledgments

I would like to thank the editors of this volume for the helpful advice and criticism. Funding was provided by the Social Sciences and Humanities Research Council of Canada. All defects are my own.

References

Alberta Environment. 2002. *South Saskatchewan River Basin Water Management Plan: Phase One, Water Allocation Transfers*, Publication No. T/661. Edmonton, AB: Alberta Environment.

Alberta Environment. 2003. *Water for Life: Alberta's Strategy for Sustainability*, Publication No. I/955. Edmonton, AB: Alberta Environment.

Alberta Water Council. 2007. *Review of Implementation Progress of Water for Life, 2005-2006.* Edmonton, AB: Alberta Water Council.

Annear, T. C., Chisholm, I., Beecher, H., Locke, A., Aarrestad, P., Burkhart, N., Coomer, C., Estes, C., Hunt, J., Jacobson, R., Jobsis, G., Kauffman, J., Marshall, J., Mayes, K., Stalnaker, C., and Wentworth., R. 2002. *Instream Flows for Riverine Resource Stewardship.* Cheyenne, WY: Instream Flow Council.

Armstrong, C., Evenden, M., and Nelles, H. 2009. *The River Returns: An Environmental History of the Bow.* Montreal, QC and Kingston, ON: McGill-Queen's University Press.

Asch, M. 2014. *On Being Here to Stay: Treaties and Aboriginal Rights in Canada.* Toronto, ON: University of Toronto Press.

Bakker, K. J., and Cameron, D. 2005. Governance, Business Models and Restructuring Water Supply Utilities: Recent Developments in Ontario, Canada. *Water Policy* 7(5): 485-508.

Barkley, P. W., and Seckler, D. W. 1972. *Economic Growth and Environmental Decay: The Solution Becomes the Problem*, Harbrace Series in Business and Economics. New York, NY: Harcourt Brace Jovanovich.

Benidickson, J. 2007. *The Culture of Flushing: A Social and Legal History of Sewage.* Vancouver, BC: UBC Press.

Blackbourn, D. 2006. *The Conquest of Nature: Water, Landscape, and the Making of Modern Germany.* New York, NY: W.W. Norton & Company.

Boyd, D. 2003. *Unnatural Law: Rethinking Canadian Environmental Law and Policy.* Vancouver, BC: UBC Press.

Breton, A. 1985. *Supplementary Statement.* In "Report of the Royal Commission on the Economic Union and Development Prospects for Canada." Vol. 3. Ottawa, ON: Minister of Supply and Services Canada.

Brown, P. G. 2008. *The Commonwealth of Life: Economics for a Flourishing Earth.* 2nd ed. Montreal, QC: Blackrose Books.

Brown, P. G., and Schmidt, J. J., eds. 2010. *Water Ethics: Foundational Readings for Students and Professionals*. Washington, D.C.: Island Press.

Cantin Cumyn, M. 2007. The Legal Status of Water in Quebec. *Quebc Studies* 42: 7-15.

Cohen, A. *From Water to Watershed: An Analysis of Rescaled Water Governance in Canada*. Unpublished Ph.D. Dissertation, University of British Columbia, Dept. of Geography, 2011.

Cohen, A. 2012. Watersheds as Boundary Objects: Scale at the Intersection of Competing Ideologies. *Environment and Planning A* 44(9): 2207-24.

Coulthard, G. S. 2014. *Red Skin, White Masks: Rejecting the Colonial Politics of Recognition*, Indigenous America. Minneapolis, MN: University of Minnesota Press.

Creighton, D. G. 2002. *The Commercial Empire of the St. Lawrence: A Study in Commerce and Politics*. 2nd ed. Toronto, ON: University of Toronto Press.

Delli Priscoli, J. 2000. Water and Civilization: Using History to Reframe Water Policy Debates and to Build a New Ecological Realism. *Water Policy* 1(6): 623-36.

Desbiens, C. 2004. Producing North and South: A Political Geography of Hydro Development in Québec. *The Canadian Geographer* 48(2): 101-18.

Desbiens, C. 2007. "Water All around, You Cannot Even Drink": The Scaling of Water in the James Bay/Eeyou Istchee. *Area* 39(3): 259-67.

Desbiens, C. 2013. *Power from the North: Territory, Identity, and the Culture of Hydroelectricity in Quebec*. Vancouver, BC: UBC Press.

Dietz, T., Fitzgerald, A., and Shwom, R. 2005. Environmental Values. *Annual Review of Environment and Resources* 30: 335-72.

Durant, R. F., Fiorino, D. J., and O'Leary, R. 2004. *Environmental Governance Reconsidered: Challenges, Choices, and Opportunities*. Cambridge, MA: The MIT Press.

Espelund, W. N. 1998. *The Struggle for Water: Politics, Rationality, and Identity in the American Southwest*. Chicago, IL: University of Chicago Press.

Feldman, D. L. 1995. *Water Resources Management: In Search of an Environmental Ethic*. Baltimore, MD: John Hopkins University Press.

Folke, C. 2003. Freshwater for Resilience: A Shift in Thinking. *Philosophical Transactions of the Royal Society of London. Series B: Biological Sciences* 358(1440): 2027-36.

Gaard, G. 2001. Women, Water, Energy: An Ecofeminist Approach. *Organization & Environment* 14(2): 157-72.

Glenn, J. 1999. *Once Upon an Oldman: Special Interest Politics and the Oldman River Dam.* Vancouver, BC: UBC Press.

Glenn, J. M. 2010. Crown Ownership of Water in Situ in Common Law Canada: Public Trusts, Classical Trusts and Fiduciary Duties. *Les Cahiers de Droit* 51(3-4): 493-519.

Groenfeldt, D., and Schmidt, J. J. 2013. Ethics and Water Governance. *Ecology and Society*. http://www.ecologyandsociety.org/vol18/iss1/art14/.

Hanemann, W. M. 2006. *The Economic Conception of Water.* In "Water Crisis: Myth or Reality?," eds. Rogers, P. P., Llamas, M. R. and Martinez-Cortina, L. London: Taylor and Francis.

Heinmiller, B. T. 2013. Advocacy Coalitions and the Alberta Water Act. *Canadian Journal of Political Science* 46(3): 525-47.

Hessing, M., Howlett, M., and Summerville, T. 2005. *Canadian Natural Resource and Environmental Policy: Political Economy and Public Policy.* 2nd ed. Vancouver, BC: UBC Press.

International Joint Commission (IJC). 2009. *The International Watersheds Initiative: Implementing a New Paradigm for Transboundary Basins. Third Report to Governments on the International Watersheds Initiative.* Available from http://www.ijc.org/en_/Reports_and_Publications.

Ioris, A. A. R. 2012. The Positioned Construction of Water Values: Pluralism, Positionality and Praxis. *Environmental Values* 21(2): 143-62.

Kay, J. J. 2000. *Ecosystems as Self-Organizing Holarchic Open Systems: Narratives and the Second Law of Thermodynamics.* In "Handbook of Ecosystem Theories and Management," eds. Jørgensen, S. E. and Müller, F. Boca Raton, FL: CRC Press – Lewis Publishers. 135-60.

Kennett, S. A. 1992. The Design of Federalism and Water Resource Management in Canada. *Research Paper No. 31* Institute of Intergovernmental Relations, Queen's University.

Kysar, D. A. 2010. *Regulating from Nowhere: Environmental Law and the Search for Objectivity.* New Haven, CT: Yale University Press.

LaSelva, S. V. 1996. *The Moral Foundations of Canadian Federalism: Paradoxes, Achievements, and Tragedies of Nationhood.* Montreal, QC: McGill-Queen's University Press.

Lindblom, C. E. 1959. The Science of "Muddling Through." *Public Administration Review* 19(2): 79-88.

Manore, J. L. 2006. *Rivers as Text: From Pre-Modern to Post-Modern Understandings of Development, Technology and the Environment in Canada and Abroad.* In "A History of

Water," eds. Tvedt, T. and Oestigaard, T. 3 vols. Vol. 3 : The world of Water, Series I. New York, NY: Tauris & Co. Ltd. 229-53.

Mascarenhas, M. 2012. *Where the Waters Divide: Neoliberalism, White Privilege, and Environmental Racism in Canada*. Lanham, MD: Lexington Books.

Mason, A. 2000. *Community, Solidarity and Belonging: Levels of Community and Their Normative Significance*. Cambridge, UK: Cambridge University Press.

McGee, W. J. 1911. Principles of Water-Power Development. *Science* 34(885): 813-25.

Merchant, C. 1997. Fish First! The Changing Ethics of Ecosystem Management. *Human Ecology Review* 4(1): 25-30.

Milly, P. C. D., Betancourt, J., Falkenmark, M., Hirsch, R. M., Kundzewicz, Z. W., Lettenmaier, D. P., and Stouffer, R. J. 2008. Stationarity Is Dead: Whither Water Management? *Science* 319(5863): 573-74.

Mitchell, B., Priddle, C., Shrubsole, D., Veale, B., and Walters, D. 2014. Integrated Water Resource Management: Lessons from Conservation Authorities in Ontario. *International Journal of Water Resources Development* 30(3): 460-74.

Nelles, H. 2005. *The Politics of Development: Forests, Mines & Hydro-Electric Power in Ontario, 1849-1941*. 2nd ed. Montreal, QC: McGill-Queen's University Press.

Norgaard, R. B. 2010. Ecosystem Services: From Eye-Opening Metaphor to Complexity Blinder. *Ecological Economics* 69(6): 1219-27.

Northwest Territories (NWT). 2010. *Northern Voices, Northern Waters: NWT Water Stewardship Strategy*: Northwest Territories, Canada.

Norton, B. G. 2005. *Sustainability: A Philosophy for Adaptive Ecosystem Management*. Chicago, IL: University of Chicago Press.

Nova Scotia. 2010. *Water for Life: Nova Scotia's Water Resource Management Strategy*. Government of Nova Scotia, http://www.gov.ns.ca/nse/water.strategy/.

Orlove, B., and Caton, S. C. 2010. Water Sustainability: Anthropological Approaches and Prospects. *Annual Review of Anthropology* 39: 401-15.

Parfit, D. 2011. *On What Matters*. Vols. 1&2. New York, NY: Oxford University Press.

Parr, J. 2010. *Sensing Changes: Technologies, Environments, and the Everyday, 1953-2003*. Vancouver: UBC Press.

Pearce W. 1891. *William Pearce Papers*, University of Alberta Archives, 9/2/7/2/6.

Phare, M. A. S. 2009. *Denying the Source: The Crisis of First Nations Water Rights*. Surrey, BC: Rocky Mountain Books Ltd.

Québec. 2002. *Our Life. Our Future. Québec Water Policy*: Environnement Québec.

Sabatier, P. A., Focht, W., Lubell, M., Trachtenberg, Z., Arnold Vedlitz, and Matlock, M., eds. 2005. *Swimming Upstream: Collaborative Approaches to Watershed Management*. Cambridge, MA: The MIT Press.

Sagoff, M. 2004. *Price, Principle, and the Environment*. New York, NY: Cambridge University Press.

Sandford, R. W., and Phare., M.-A. S. 2011. *Ethical Water : Learning to Value What Matters Most*. Victoria, BC: Rocky Mountain Book Ltd.

Sax, J. L. 1994. Understanding Transfers: Community Rights and the Privatization of Water. *West-Northwest Journal of Environmental Law and Policy* 14: 33-40.

Schmidt, J. J. 2010. *Water Ethics and Water Management*. In "Water Ethics: Foundational Readings for Students and Professionals," eds. Brown, P. G. and Schmidt, J. J. Washington, D.C.: Island Press. 3-15

Schmidt, J. J. 2011. *Alternative Water Futures in Alberta. Edmonton: Parkland Institute*. Edmonton, AB: Parkland Institute. Available from http://parklandinstitute.ca/ research/summary/alternative_water_futures_in_alberta/.

Schmidt, J. J. 2014a. Historicising the Hydrosocial Cycle. *Water Alternatives* 7(1): 220-34.

Schmidt, J. J. 2014b. Water Management and the Procedural Turn: Norms and Transitions in Alberta. *Water Resources Management* 28(4): 1127-41.

Schmidt, J. J., and Peppard, C. Z. 2014. Water Ethics on a Human Dominated Planet: Rationality, Context and Values in Global Governance. *WIREs Water* 1(6): 533-47.

Schmidt, J. J., and Shrubsole, D. 2013. Modern Water Ethics: Implications for Shared Governance. *Environmental Values* 22(3): 359-79.

Schorr, D. B. 2005. Appropriation as Agrarianism: Distributive Justice in the Creation of Property Rights. *Ecology Law Quarterly* 32(1): 3-71.

Senecal, C., and Madramootoo, C. A. 2005. Watershed Management: Review of Canadian Diversity. *Water Policy* 7(5): 509-22.

Simpson, A. 2014. *Mohawk Interruptus: Political Life across the Borders of Settler States*. Durham, NC: Duke University Press.

Solomon, S. 2010. *Water: The Epic Struggle for Wealth, Power, and Civilization*. New York, NY: HarperCollins Publishers.

Sprague, J. B. 2007. *Great Wet North? Canada's Myth of Water Abundance*. In "Eau Canada: The Future of Canada's Water," ed. Bakker, K. J. Vancouver and Toronto: UBC Press. 23-35.

Taylor, C. 2004. *Modern Social Imaginaries*. Durham, NC: Duke University Press.

Tisdell, J. G. 2003. Equity and Social Justice in Water Doctrines. *Social Justice Research* 16(4): 401-16.

Tully, J. 1995. *Strange Multiplicity: Constitutionalism in an Age of Diversity*. Cambridge, UK: Cambridge University Press.

Weibust, I. 2009. *Green Leviathan: The Case for a Federal Role in Environmental Policy*. Burlington, VT: Ashgate.

White, G. F. 1969. *Strategies of American Water Management*. Ann Arbor, MI: University of Michigan Press.

Water Governance
Restoring Sustainable Use through Indigenous Values

Merrell-Ann S. Phare, LL.M
Executive Director, Centre for Indigenous Environmental Resources

Brendan Mulligan
Environmental Protection Analyst, Environment Yukon, Government of Yukon

Issues of environmental and social justice are almost always closely linked. This is particularly the case for the Indigenous people in Canada and is perhaps most clearly manifested in their current water crisis. As of August 31, 2014, there were 137 First Nations communities across Canada under a Drinking Water Advisory and this number, shockingly, has hovered at this level for years, showing no signs of decreasing (Health Canada 2012). Nearly two thousand homes within First Nations communities have no running water for drinking or flushing the toilet (Neegan Burnside 2011). Homes that are serviced by individual systems are scarcely better off. Most wells do not meet the Guidelines for Canadian Drinking Water Quality and nearly half of the septic systems have operational concerns (ibid.).

The framing of this water crisis is a critical issue because the way in which a problem is described inherently suggests a solution. Is it a technical problem (implying a technical solution), a legal problem, a problem of governance? Or is it a problem based upon something deeper, a loss of connection to water that began when Canada was colonized? In this paper it is argued that the water problems faced by Indigenous peoples in Canada are chiefly problems of history, namely a history of colonization. The legacy of colonization challenges us all, albeit from different experiences and perspectives. Understood in this way, it becomes clear that the solution to these problems begins with a collective decolonization. We feel there is a broad opportunity for the process of collective decolonization to take root among non-Indigenous Canadians as well as among Indigenous people in Canada. Collective decolonization will lead to the acceptance of a plurality of water ethics which will, in turn, foster stronger collaborations on water projects and clear a path toward a widespread commitment to water reform, including the creation of a national water strategy.

Colonialism

We know the colonial history of Canada. The European use (and in many cases forceful taking) of that lands, waters and resources that would later comprise Canada dispossessed the indigenous inhabitants. While this is not the main focus of this paper, one of the most damaging elements of colonization from the perspective of the link between environment and culture was the residential school program. Residential schools, run by the Department of Indian Affairs, were designed to implement the Canadian government's "aggressive assimilation" policy. The government's vision was that Aboriginal[1] children would learn English and adopt Christianity as well as Canadian customs. The idea being that this would cause their Indigenous traditions to diminish, or be completely abolished, in a few generations. In total, about 150,000 First Nations, Inuit and Métis children were removed from their communities and forced to attend the schools (CBC 2008). There were a total of about 130 schools located in every territory and province except Newfoundland, Prince Edward Island and New Brunswick. The earliest residential school opened in the 19th century and the last closed in 1996, just over fifteen years ago (ibid.).

The residential school program attempted, among many things, to sever the connection between Indigenous culture and Indigenous lands and waters through the forcible removal of Indigenous children from their homes to boarding schools for much of their pre-adult life. Attendance was often mandatory. In addition to the loss of language and other significant elements of culture, being physically located in a residential school ensured that Indigenous children would no longer learn the elements of their culture that were related to knowledge of the land and waters. In far too many cases it was catastrophically successful. To be colonized is to have lost or have had destroyed, in essence, the foundation of who you are as a person and as a society.

Decolonization

Decolonization, the undoing of colonialism, is most often understood culturally or politically. In Canada, many First Nations speak of the need to decolonize their thinking as well as their communities. This need usually focuses on spiritual and cultural restoration. Some speak of decolonization in the sense that they are seeking self-determination as a governance structure within their nation. This paper does not address either of those two elements of decolonization, but instead explores the idea of decolonizing our relationship to water.

---

[1] In this chapter, the terms Indigenous and Aboriginal are used interchangeably.

Fundamentally, we argue that an important aspect of decolonization entails the restoration of traditional and sustainable relations between people and the waters that sustain them, relations that have been severed.

The Dominant Ideology

In order to dismantle the colonial legacy in terms of the use of and relationship to water, or to even begin to address its negative effects, we must first understand the dominant water ideology introduced by the colonial powers. This dominant water ideology includes, but is not limited to, the following principles:

- the idea of the economy as the dominant social organizing structure;

- the idea of the environment as endlessly available and technologically malleable;

- the elimination of rights of water and nature;

- the parceling of nature into packages of rights held by humans;

- the separation of rights from a consequent sense of profound responsibility;

- the elimination of the concept that governments have a fiduciary responsibility as they hold water in trust for people and nature; and

- a creation of a hierarchy of rights among humans where the rights and worldviews of Indigenous people are less significant than those of the majority who uphold Western worldviews

Of course such a cluster of views does not hold in all places or in all situations. It is however, the predominant perspective in Canada. Particularly in the halls of power, traditional indigenous worldviews, which recognize and revere the interconnectedness of all life with water, appear poorly understood. They are all but absent in Canadian water policy. The assumption seems to be that the "western world" is on a singular, one-dimensional path to progress that is supported by all and that this progress has advanced beyond indigenous worldviews by means of superior technology and ideology.

The dominant water ideology comprises a set of principles that, in some circles, are taken to be natural laws, or at least seen as the only reasonable set of principles governing our actions with respect to water. Of course, in reality, they are but one set of principles in a wide spectrum of possibilities. There are many challenges on the path to decolonization. One of the first to confront is the challenge of dismantling the dominant water ideology and recognizing alternative principles that might lead to greater environmental and social justice for all beneficiaries of the water cycle including people, plants, animals and ecosystems.

We argue that facing this challenge is essential to the long-term sustainability of water, as well as the social relations that are sustained by water. This challenge can therefore be interpreted as a broad social opportunity for sustainability and social justice.

An Indigenous Voice: Lessons from an Elder

"It took us 500 years to get into this situation and it will take us 500 years to get out of it."

> – Leanne Simpson, writer and scholar of Michi Saagiik Nishnaabeg ancestry, retelling the words of an Elder

There are at least two key lessons we can draw from the wisdom relayed by Leanne Simpson. First, all cultures in Canada, Indigenous and non-Indigenous, have strayed to one extent or another from a deep understanding of the significance of water, and all elements of the environment, to the ongoing health and sustainability of all living and non-living entities.

The second message we might take from the above quote is that while patience is required in addressing the challenges we face, so is immediate action. Fortunately, there are many champions of Indigenous water ethics that are currently working hard to practice sustainable water governance. Their success in focusing attention on critical water issues is a source of great optimism.

The Case for Optimism

The sustainable water governance of the future is actually already being practiced today. A few examples demonstrate the beginnings of this movement.

There is positive movement towards a First Nations National Water Strategy which would be inclusive of an Indigenous Commission on Water. The idea of such a commission was recommended in the Report of the Expert Panel on Safe Drinking Water for First Nations (Willms and Shier 2006) and supported by the Assembly of First Nations (AFN 2008). The Commission would be an institution created by and for Indigenous Peoples to gather information, provide analysis, educate the public and support Indigenous advocacy on issues related to water and wastewater in Canada (AFN 2012).

The groundbreaking Northwest Territories Water Stewardship Strategy, "Northern Voices, Northern Waters" serves as a model for decolonizing hydro-social relations (NWT 2010). The Strategy was developed in partnership with indigenous governments and aims to guide effective long-term stewardship of the Territory's water resources. The appropriate use and consideration of all types of knowledge, including traditional, local and western scientific, are an integral part of the Strategy and related initiative (ibid.).

In 2006, the Keepers of the Water, a family of regional, community-based Keepers organizations and watershed gathering committees was established. Keepers of the Water began with a gathering of Elders from the north who met on the shores of the great Deh Cho (Mackenzie River) in 2006. The gathering was called because the people of the northern Mackenzie River Basin were becoming alarmed with reports of increased turbidity and toxicity and a decrease in the volume of water in their watershed (Keepers of the Water 2012). The Keepers continue to meet and work together to "protect water for all living things today and tomorrow" (ibid.).

A well-publicized example of the decolonization of water in North America is Josephine Mandamin's Mother Earth Water Walk. The walk includes two Anishinawbe Grandmothers and a group of Anishinawbe Women and Men who have been raising awareness of critical water issues by walking the perimeter of the Great Lakes (Mother Earth Water Walk 2012). Along with a group of supporters, they walked around Lake Superior in Spring of 2003, around Lake Michigan in 2004, Lake Huron in 2005, Lake Ontario in 2006 and Lake Erie in 2007. The walk continues each year and has created other similar initiatives across Canada, such as Katherine Morrisseau-Sinclair's Lake Winnipeg Water Walk 2014 (Morrisseau-Sinclair 2014).

There are many legal cases on Indigenous water rights being asserted in the courts. These cases, along with several watershed planning initiatives led by Indigenous Peoples, illustrate how decolonization of relations between Indigenous peoples and waters in Canada is being developed through legal and administrative mechanisms (e.g. Phare 2009).

All of these initiatives are Indigenous-led and governance-related and most of them are being carried out in partnership with, or with the involvement of, non-Indigenous peoples and/or organizations. It is encouraging to see that both Indigenous and non-Indigenous cultures have very effective pockets of activity directed at reconnecting to the fundamental understanding that water is significant to all life. The examples cited above suggest that the sustainable water governance of the future is starting to be practiced today, though perhaps the interconnections between various initiatives are not yet obvious. These activities may be considered initial strands weaving themselves into a loose fabric of water governance reform, from the ground up. They are based on Indigenous worldviews, or a profound recognition by non-Indigenous others that

Indigenous worldviews have the ability to contribute in a very meaningful way to the reform of Canada's water policy.

The Need for True Collaboration

This new way of approaching water governance is truly collaborative. This approach is characterized not by governments debating the existence and scope of their jurisdictions over water, but rather on an understanding that in most situations three levels of government (federal, provincial, and indigenous) and in some cases four (with the addition of municipal government) are indeed necessary to ensure that waters are protected and used in a truly sustainable way. All levels of government are needed not only because they have legitimate powers to ensure that water policy and governance reform is implemented, but also because they each come with a set of embedded values that must be understood in order to create a sustainable model of water governance for all participants.

If all governments listed above were consistently at the table and were committed to true collaboration in achieving sustainable water governance, the model that would be created could best be described as collaborative ecological governance. Ecological governance necessarily involves not only a set of outcomes but also a process of re-evaluating one's relationship to the environment. Such outcomes include, but are not limited to, systems thinking and interconnectedness, water for nature and precaution. Each of these are values that are predominant in Indigenous traditional worldviews on water and nature. This process is fundamental in order to redirect ourselves away from the singular path that we have been heading down for too long.

The Way Forward: Reconciliation

"Let us face it, we are all here to stay."

– Chief Justice Lamer in Delgamuukw v. B.C., Dec. 11, 1997

It is commonly understood that Aboriginal rights exist and are recognized and affirmed under section 35 of the Constitution of Canada (The Constitution Act 1867). This recognition creates certain protections for Aboriginal people. Many legal cases have resulted from the failure of Canadian governments to adequately address potential impacts on Aboriginal rights as a result of government decision-making.

What is rarely discussed is what the Supreme Court of Canada (SCC) claims to be the point of the inherent protections and recognitions under section 35. The

SCC emphasizes, in most aboriginal rights cases, the need for our societies to achieve reconciliation. They link the idea of reconciliation to all elements of Aboriginal rights recognition and protection. In doing this they are implying that we do not merely protect Aboriginal rights and limit their infringement because the law tells us to do so.

It must be noted that, at their core, Aboriginal rights are fundamentally environmental rights, as most Aboriginal rights are directly and indirectly connected to functioning ecosystems. Almost every Aboriginal rights case begins with a decision by a non-Aboriginal government to use some element of the environment in some way that is harmful to that environment. So, the SCC implores us, in our decision-making concerning the use of the environment, to consider the broader context within which rights operate in our society and to find a way to achieve just and ethical reconciliation.

This broad need to reconcile relationships exists at many levels. We must reconcile the colonial relationships of our past, our current colonial relationships with nature and, if we fail to alter our course for the better, there will be a need to reconcile our colonial relationship with the future. If this reconciliation goal is explicit in our water governance structures, all cultures can find cultural and environmental renewal. This represents a tremendous social opportunity for all Canadians.

Oliver Brandes, of the University of Victoria's POLIS Project on Ecological Governance has stated that "in the next five to ten years, water and watershed governance is going to have to change more than it has in the last 200 years" (Water Canada 2012). One of the fundamental driving forces of this change must be recognition by all people in Canada that the founding cultures of these lands, the Indigenous cultures, have within them certain fundamental truths that can and should guide us through our current period of crisis and beyond. Chief amongst these fundamental truths is our collective need to decolonize in terms of our relationship with water and to restore a primary relationship within which we choose to make decisions based on what is in the best long-term interests of water in its natural state.

Envisioning a New Decolonized Water Ethic

As we confront the enormity of the water challenges facing us in the 21st century, we should not sacrifice higher visionary ideals for short-term practicality. Water decolonization will necessitate deep change that begins with asking ourselves questions we are not generally accustomed to asking. Exploring the broad scope of decolonized water ethics could be guided by reflection on many diverse questions that affect every aspect of our lives, including the following:

- In our legal and political systems...

    - ...could rights that we currently ignore, such as rights for nature and Indigenous water rights, be recognised?

    - ...could we acknowledge the existence of different jurisdictions and authorities that acknowledge the significance of water?

    - ...could legal decisions be determined based upon the extent to which the outcome was in line with our water ethics?

    - ...could "water use decisions" be based on a precautionary approach and decisions to "reform" water decision-making be undertaken with courage?

    - ...could policies become true statements of commitment to which we hold ourselves accountable to ensure we honour the sacredness of water in our world?

    - ...could the laws we have reverse liabilities, responsibilities, punishments, deterrents, and burdens of proof when it comes to how we use, protect and restore water?

- Would our economic systems and analyses be based upon recognizing limits, ensuring preservation and restoration and a goal of sufficiency and happiness rather than maximum shareholder return on investment?

- In our education system, what information about the world and our future would we teach our children? Could water ethics form the basis of engineering, business, law and medical school curricula?

- In our medical system, on what would we focus our research and our efforts? Would the only acceptable medicines be those that do not harm water?

- Roughly one-third of food produced for human consumption is lost or wasted globally (FAO 2011); how would we change how we use water to grow, transport, discard and share food?

- In the realm of music and art, what would we consider beautiful in the world? Would water be seen as one of the most sacredly beautiful entities the world has known?

- And finally, love: who and what would we love in the world and how would we demonstrate it? How would we demonstrate love of nature and water?

Conclusion

Indigenous Peoples in Canada have been in a process of decolonization for so long that they have much to teach non-Indigenous peoples about how it is done. It is rarely recognized that all Canadians have been colonized by an ideology of water commodification, waste and unsustainable technological adaptation and that therefore the opportunities presented by decolonization apply to all Canadians. This recognition is one of the most significant barriers preventing a widespread commitment to water reform, and this paper was intended to suggest that we begin a very deep and complex process to address this need. The path will be brighter if we all recognize, accept and embrace a traditional Indigenous water ethic based on restoring, preserving and preventing harm to the connection that we as humans, and all other entities, have to water.

References

AFN. 2008. *Resolution No. 50/2008: Indigenous Commission on Water*. AFN Special Chiefs Assembly, Ottawa, ON, December 9-11.

AFN. 2012. *Strategy to Protect and Advance Indigenous Water Rights*. 33rd Annual General Assembly [Powerpoint in possession of the author]: Assembly of First Nations.

CBC News. 2008. *A History of Residential Schools in Canada*. CBC/Radio-Canada, http://www.cbc.ca/news/canada/story/2008/05/16/f-faqs-residential-schools.html.

Delgamuukw v. B.C. 1997. 3 S.C.R. 1010.

FAO. 2011. *Global Food Losses and Food Waste: Extent, Causes and Prevention*. Rome, IT: Food and Agriculture Organization of the United Nations. Available from http://www.fao.org/ag/ags/ags-division/publications/publication/en/c/74045/

Health Canada. 2012. *First Nations, Inuit and Aboriginal Health: Drinking Water and Wastewater*. Health Canada/Santé Canada, http://www.hc-sc.gc.ca/fniah-spnia/promotion/public-publique/water-eau-eng.php.

Keepers of the Water. 2012. *Keeping the Arctic Ocean Basin*. Keepers of the Water, http://www.keepersofthewater.ca.

Morrisseau-Sinclair, K. 2014. *Lake Winnipeg Water Walk 2014*. http://lakewinnipegwaterwalk.ca/a-personal-statement-to-help-you-understand-my-passion-katherine-morrisseau-sinclair/.

Mother Earth Water Walk. 2012. http://www.motherearthwaterwalk.com.

Neegan Burnside Ltd. 2011. *National Assessment of First Nations Water and Wastewater Systems: National Roll-up Report.* [Report prepared for the Department of Indian and Northern Affairs, Canada].

Northwest Territories (NWT). 2010. *Northern Voices, Northern Waters: NWT Water Stewardship Strategy:* Northwest Territories, Canada.

Phare, M. A. S. 2009. *Denying the Source: The Crisis of First Nations Water Rights.* Surrey, BC: Rocky Mountain Books Ltd.

The Constitution Act, 1867 (UK), 30 & 31 Victoria, c 3.

Water Canada. 2012. *Water's Next 2012.* Water Canada, http://watercanada.net/2013/polis-water-sustainability-project/.

Willms & Shier Environmental Lawyers LLP. 2006. *Report of the Expert Panel on Safe Drinking Water for First Nations Volume II: Legal Analysis.* Ottawa, ON: Minister of Public Works and Government Services Canada [Report prepared for the Minister of Indian Affairs and Northern Development].

Water as a Governance Opportunity

Alice Cohen, Ph.D.
Assistant Professor, Acadia University

This chapter explores the relationship between governance and water in the Canadian context by asking two interrelated questions: what are the governance opportunities for water and, what opportunities or lessons can water create for governance more generally?

In asking these questions, the chapter contributes to two ongoing conversations. The first of these conversations stems from thinking in environmental geography and seeks to better understand the way that societies organize themselves in relation to the natural, or non-human, world. Where do we draw the line between these two worlds, and what impact does that line-drawing have on our decision-making? Perhaps more importantly, how do our existing decision-making frameworks reflect, work with, or even contradict the biophysical realities of the resources they seek to govern?

The second conversation relates to questions regarding shared, or delegated, water governance arrangements. Before proceeding, a working definition of "governance" is helpful. The distinction between "government" and "governance" draws on trends observed through the 1990s that saw a proliferation of actors involved in decision-making processes and service delivery schemes that were once the exclusive purview of centralized governments (Kettl 2000; Peters and Pierre 1998; Rhodes 1996; Salamon and Elliott 2002). As such, I use the term "governance" to denote a broad range of decision-making arrangements, of which government-led, top-down decision-making is only one of many. In the Canadian context, the Institute on Governance defines governance as "a process whereby societies or organizations make their important decisions, determine whom they involve in the process and how they render account" (Graham et al. 2003). Thus, in the context of water, water governance can be defined as follows:

"Water governance is the range of political, organizational and administrative processes through which communities articulate their interests, their input is absorbed, decisions are made and implemented, and decision makers are held accountable in the development and management of water resources and delivery of water services. It is distinct from

water management, which is the operational, on-the ground activity to regulate water and impose conditions on its use." (Nowlan and Bakker 2010, 7)

The relationship between water issues and governance issues often pivots around the concept of good governance. Attention is paid especially to good governance within water-related institutions as well as to changes in water-related institutions undertaken in the name of better governance (Allan and Wouters 2004; Bakker 2003; Grindle 2007). What constitutes good governance has been extensively debated. An emerging consensus states that the principals of good governance include *inter alia*, participation, inclusiveness, gender equity, fairness, rule of law, transparency, accountability, legitimacy, consensus orientation, responsiveness, resilience, connectivity, effectiveness, efficiency, strategic vision, direction, and performance (Batterbury and Fernando 2006; European Commission 2003; Lockwood 2010). Principles of good governance are most often applied in the context of international development, particularly in relation to lending conditions from International Financial Institutions (See Andrews 2008; Doornbos 2001; Grindle 2004; Nanda 2006). These principals are also used when responding to water-related questions, both internationally and in Canada (Bakker 2003; Rogers and Hall 2003; Turton et al. 2007). In such circumstances, stakeholder engagement and transparency are especially important. Recent work on delegated water governance in Canada suggests that power-sharing arrangements can be described using two spectrums, one describing the division of delegated decision-making power among those sharing power and another describing the degree of participation by various stakeholders (Nowlan and Bakker 2007 and 2010; NRTEE 2011).

Figure 1 illustrates these two spectrums and highlights the range of decision-making arrangements that constitute what are typically thought of as "water governance." Many of the challenges and opportunities in the Canadian water governance landscape are related to these two spectra.

In addition to hosting a range of water governance arrangements, water governance in Canada has been critiqued for, among other things, a federal lack of coordination (Bakker 2007), failure to protect Canadian waters from the (real or perceived) threat of bulk water exports (Christensen 2011; Quinn 2007), poor collection and management of water quality and quantity data (Dunn and Bakker 2011), weak drinking water quality standards (Christensen 2011) – especially with respect to First Nations (Eggertson 2008; von der Porten and de Loë 2010) – lack of interprovincial coordination and federal leadership (Bakker and Cook 2011), insufficient research – especially with respect to groundwater (Senate of Canada 2005) – and lax enforcement at both the federal (Amos et al. 2011; Boyd 2003) and provincial levels.

                    Water as a Governance Opportunity

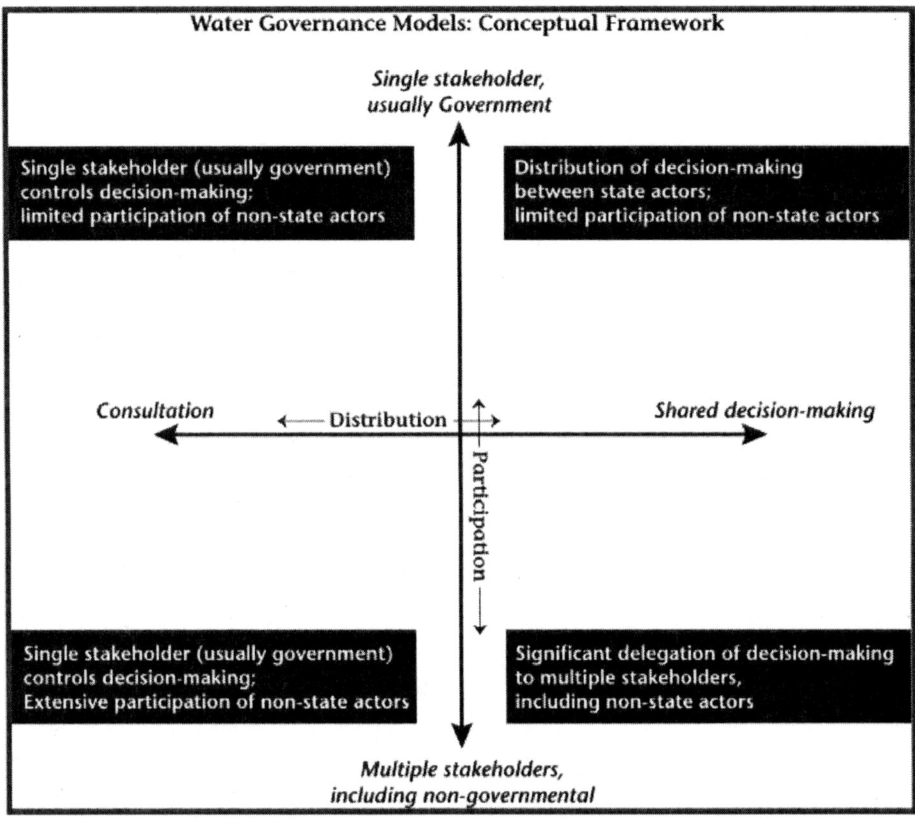

Source: Image reproduced with permission from Nowlan and Bakker (2007).

The Opportunities

Returning to the questions of governance opportunities for water and, what governance arrangements can learn from decades of water management, the opportunities listed below aim to take on a different tone and to look for toeholds into positive change. In so doing, I do not intend to make light of the grave challenges facing Canadian water governance in the coming years; the problems are serious, immediate, and must be addressed. Many of these challenges are not new. A read of the 1987 Canadian Water Policy shows the reader how little has changed in twenty-five years. However, in addition to working towards breaking down known policy challenges, we perhaps need to seek new ways to work around them In other words, we know what the problems are; how can we work around them to breathe new life into what many have argued is a broken system? Three possible innovations are discussed below.

Re-framing the Nature-Society Relationship

One opportunity arises from the possibility of rethinking the relationship between the human and non-human worlds. When discussing this relationship, geographers often refer to the nature-society binary (e.g. Braun and Castree 2001; Whatmore 1999) wherein a barrier exists between the realms of the human and the non-human. We know, of course, that this distinction is an artificial one, and water is an especially integrative substance as it literally flows into, out of, and through biophysical systems and individual organisms (both human and non-human). Yet we continue to adhere to, and even create, regulations, institutions, and boundaries that continuously reinforce an artificial divide between the two. To give a recent example of this phenomenon in action, Cohen and Harris (2014) looked at the way in which watersheds are governed in four different Canadian provinces and argued that by defining watersheds as "natural," or as "nature's boundaries," other spaces of engagement (Cox 1998) become, *de facto*, human. These other spaces were most often the spaces that we traditionally think of when we think of environmental governance: municipalities and provinces. The end result is that watersheds, and by association watershed-scale organizations and governance initiatives, become a space wherein activities related to nature take place: such as stream cleanups, public outreach, education about environmental issues and scientific data collection. There is nothing wrong with these activities, in fact they are critical. However, by framing watersheds as natural, we relegate the more human elements of environmental action to other scales – namely the municipal and provincial levels. It is at these scales that we make decisions about human activity: licensing, zoning, permitting, and so on are done outside of the watershed scale. Cordoning off "watersheds" as a separate sphere of activity can therefore have the unintentional consequence of reinforcing the nature-society binary. In other words, by defining particular spaces (i.e. watersheds) as "natural" and other spaces (i.e. municipal and provincial) as "human," we are creating a divide in a relationship that many of us instinctively know to be intimately intertwined, interconnected, and, particularly in the case of water, interdependent.

There exist tremendous opportunities here. What might it look like to have policy that explicitly recognizes the connections between the human and non-human worlds, and that actively seeks to overcome the institutional barriers to their integration? One possibility is to create innovative policy that integrates water quality and human health. For example, Pentland (this volume) discusses widespread concern around evidence suggesting increasing numbers (and volumes) of new pollutants in our waterways, especially those categorized as Pharmaceuticals and Personal Care Products (PPCPs). Is the solution to this ever-increasing suite of contaminants to filter them out at the water treatment site or to develop technologies to remove them before entering the waterways, perhaps in the sewage system itself? Other possible solutions include incentives to return unused prescription medication for proper disposal, to question the use of these products in the first place and to conduct research that focuses on the health effects of PPCPs once they become environmental contaminants.

Breaking Down Silos

A second governance opportunity for water lies in breaking down the kind of "silo thinking" that consistently permeates much of our thinking surrounding water in Canada. This is not a new idea. The concept of fragmentation in particular has been the focus of much attention in the Canadian context (e.g. Bakker and Cook 2011). Fragmented governance in the Canadian context is often attributed to the division of powers under the 1867 *Constitution Act,* which is silent on the question of responsibility for water specifically, but allocates responsibility for natural resources in general to the provinces (see section 92 (a) of the *Act*). This creates a political climate wherein the federal government has little incentive to act on water (and indeed, environmental) issues (Bakker and Cook 2011; Harrison 1996; Paehlke 2000). Lack of federal involvement is an ongoing issue raised by commentators on Canadian water policy (mostly outside of Quebec). Federal governments of all stripes have come under fire for their reluctance to adopt pan-Canadian drinking water quality standards (Hill and Harrison 2006; Eggertson 2008; Hill et al. 2008), to explicitly exempt bulk water exports (Quinn 2007), to adequately fund water research, collect and store data on water quality and quantity (Dunn and Bakker 2011) and, as is discussed later in this chapter, to enforce existing federal regulations prohibiting pollution in fish-bearing waterways (Boyd 2003; Amos et al. 2011). In these areas, lack of federal leadership is often traced to a combination of fragmented water governance and lack of political will on the part of the federal government. The issue of fragmentation is circular in that fragmentation as both the cause and effect of lack of federal leadership.

Despite the fact that much has been written about fragmentation elsewhere, I raise it here to point out that many of the ideas in this volume could be implemented in efforts to escape the fragmentation-lack-of-leadership circular argument. In other words, rather than working to break down what some argue is a dysfunctional federal-provincial environmental relationship, we might seek instead to bring new actors into the mix in innovative ways or to carve out spaces where meaningful inter-jurisdictional collaboration can occur.

For example, Furlong (this volume) emphasizes the importance of holistic approaches to municipal water governance rather than separating water service delivery from other municipal services. Fragmentation within municipal government is an example of the kind of problem that if remedied could have the potential to make a significant difference. However, this idea has received little attention in national water policy dialogues, which, as above, have typically focused on the jurisdictions of the federal and provincial governments (e.g. Cook 2011). Recently, the Federation of Canadian Municipalities (FCM) has turned to this integrated approach, offering a potential example of collaboration within a particular governance level.

Additional opportunities for overcoming fragmentation can be found through meaningful collaboration with Aboriginal communities (see Phare, this volume). Cape Breton's Collaborative Environmental Planning Initiative (CEPI), for example, is committed to what they call "two-eyed seeing." Two-eyed seeing means to have "one eye on our past history and teachings, and one eye on modern science" (CEPI 2011, 10). The group has also placed the Mi'kmaq Medicine Wheel at the heart of its charter (See Figure 2). As elaborated below, the Medicine Wheel represents balance between four different quadrants. This balance is the foundational belief for the charter, which aims to protect the Bras d'Or Lakes on Cape Breton Island and has been signed by Aboriginal and non-Aboriginal leaders. The signatories include First Nations chiefs, representatives from relevant municipalities, and deputy ministers from federal and provincial agencies.

The four quadrants of the Mi'kmaq medicine wheel represent physical, mental, emotional, and spiritual elements, and serves to remind decision-makers that a balance must be struck among these four elements. Indeed, as the CEPI charter notes, "no decision should be made based solely on one element of the Medicine Wheel, while understanding and embracing the need to take a well-rounded approach to everything we do. Everything has to be balanced across the four quadrants" (CEPI 2011, 17).

In addition to presenting fresh thinking with regard to fragmentation issues that have hindered federal and provincial governments for over a century, many Aboriginal groups do not recognize the political boundaries that divide their territories, thereby rendering moot the question of jurisdictional fragmentation. On the Pacific coast, for example, Coast Salish people have worked together to identify and re-connect with coastal lands and waters that were divided through European map-drawing exercises (Norman 2012). Through activities such as renaming the boundary waters as the Salish Sea (Rose-Redwood 2011), Coast Salish people on both sides of the Canada-US border have prompted a re-thinking of what constitutes a political boundary. Perhaps more importantly, this reframing shines a spotlight on what some of the actual implications of boundary

Figure 2: Charter for the Bras d'Or Lakes

drawing are and, in so doing, brings to light alternate narratives of fragmentation. In other words, stepping back and questioning how our jurisdictions are constructed and analyzing what assumptions and prejudices are embedded in our system of boundary-making might create a pathway around the fragmentation issue in Canada.

Lastly, Findlay (this volume) addresses how "off the radar" groups can bring together individuals with different backgrounds and interests to work around the "silo thinking" of their home institutions by coming up with innovative solutions to complex problems. In other words, if governmental departments at any level are engaging in turf wars, or, conversely and more commonly, buck-passing, it seems a promising alternative is to take the conversation off the public stage. This approach is unquestionably at the low end of the public participation spectrum (see Fig. 1), but that is perhaps its virtue. In some cases smaller groups of representatives meeting informally or formally behind closed doors can result in more effective discussions because this creates a "safe space" where relevant persons can discuss contentious issues and come up with innovative solutions before presenting ideas to policy-makers and the public.

Thinking Outside the Policy

A third opportunity relates to the idea of a national water policy, mentioned both throughout this book and the subject of much study and advocacy elsewhere. The last decade has seen significant pressures to this effect. In 2007, the Gordon Group of Concerned Scientists and Citizens developed *Changing the Flow: A Blueprint for Federal Action on Freshwater*. The report was grounded in principles of conservation and centered around a citizen vision and a watershed-based governance system. The report highlighted the lack of federal capacity in many water-related areas and called on the federal government to act on recommendations provided in the report (Morris et al. 2007). In 2007, the federal government committed to the creation of a national water strategy but there has been no follow-through (Clarke 2008). The following year, Dr. Rob de Loë worked in collaboration with the Canadian Water Resources Association to reinforce calls for a national water strategy (de Loë 2008a, 2008b and 2009). Despite these and other calls, Canadians are still waiting for their national water policy.

Although no one can deny the utility of such a policy, I suggest that a national or federal water policy need not be the holy grail of all water governance in Canada. Looking outside of this policy presents at least two additional governance opportunities. First, we must work with what we already have. A national policy would no doubt enhance current efforts, but there exists such a tremendous gap between what already exists in the Canadian water policy arsenal and what is being done that we could accomplish a great deal simply by acting on and enforcing those policies and regulations that already exist. As outlined in the introduction to this chapter, good governance literature reiterates the importance of transparency, monitoring and enforcement. In light of these principles, the following is an illustration of what it might look like to act on what we already have.

As mentioned above, one area that we could make better use of existing legislation relates to engagement with First Nations communities. The 1997 Delgamuukw case (*Delgammukw v. British Columbia*) clarified the duty of government to consult with potentially affected Aboriginal people in matters relating to environmental issues. The *Delgammukw* judgment reads:

"The right to choose to what uses land can be put, subject to the ultimate limit that those uses cannot destroy the ability of the land to sustain future generations of Aboriginal peoples, suggests that the fiduciary relationship between the Crown and Aboriginal peoples may be satisfied by the involvement of Aboriginal peoples in decisions taken with respect to their lands. There is always a duty of consultation and, in most cases, the duty will be significantly deeper than mere consultation." (Delgamuukw v. British Columbia, (1997) 3 S.C.R. 1010, emphasis added).

The *Delgamuukw* decision emphasizes that Canada's Aboriginal people are "not just another stakeholder" (NAFA 2000) and that there must be more meaningful engagement between Aboriginal communities and all levels of governments. This means that engagement with Aboriginal communities does not fit cleanly into the axes of participation and delegation outlined in the introduction to this chapter. Nevertheless, more meaningful engagement between Aboriginal communities and all levels of government can serve both as an opportunity in and of itself and as a vehicle for deeper transformation of Canada's water governance models, an idea that is outlined elsewhere in this volume.

Another arguably underused tool in the Canadian water governance toolbox is Canada's 1987 Water Policy, which discusses the need "to produce legislative provisions to address inter-jurisdictional water issues relating to levels, flows, and quality, [to] ensure the effectiveness of regulatory measures through the provision of appropriate enforcement and compliance measures, [to] ensure that the public is consulted and that its views are considered in all major federal water management decisions, [and to] encourage and support opportunities for public consultation and participation in integrated planning" (Environment Canada, 1987, 5-9). The issues we are wrestling with today are not new. Therefore, in addition to putting our energies toward creating a new policy, we may also be wise to look back and supplement our calls for new policies with calls to act on the policies we already have. We have a long way to go, but perhaps starting with existing legislation and policy presents a good starting point.

The journey to a revised and updated national water policy presents an opportunity in and of itself. The very process of working through what such a policy might entail is a chance to take on some of the broad opportunities mentioned elsewhere. It might, for example, offer an opportunity to re-think the relationships between the ethical and the political. Schmidt (this volume) discusses this idea further. Integrating the ethical into the political in the form of a national water policy might include dialogue and public debate about questions that mainstream water policy has not confronted directly. What is the relationship, for example, between a right to water and water licensing processes? What kinds of priorities are reflected in existing licensing structures? Are those priorities ones we agree with? Who is privileged through existing water use structures, and who is not? Conversations around such a policy could also seek to work through some of the issues that Merrell-Ann Phare raises in this volume and elsewhere. Perhaps most importantly, such conversations could exemplify the kinds of new and productive relationships between indigenous and non-indigenous people that are required in order to create truly innovative, integrative and just policies.

Tragic events in the northern Ontario Aboriginal community of Attawapiskat provide an example of the new kinds of thinking that could be shaping our water policy. In the fall of 2011, Chief Theresa Spence declared a state of emergency in response to deplorable living conditions in the community. These conditions included overcrowding, toxic mold, and lack of clean drinking water and sanitation services (CBC 2011; Scoffield 2011). Bringing these issues to the table in discussing a national water policy could highlight both the integrative approach discussed by Kathryn Furlong in her chapter (this volume) and important questions surrounding Aboriginal sovereignty and health. Sticking with the Attawapiskat example, we might think about policy options that integrate water infrastructure with housing policy and about governance mechanisms that recognize that equal outcomes do not necessarily mean equal treatment. All of these activities speak back to the possibility of using the journey towards a national water policy as an opportunity in and of itself, particularly for breaking down the perceived dichotomy between bottom up and top down approaches to policy-making. Thinking through these kinds of questions could be undertaken in the name of the development of a national water policy, but the policy itself need not be the end goal.

Conclusion

This chapter has sought to identify opportunities at the intersection of governance and water in the Canadian context. The ideas expressed here bring together opportunities highlighted elsewhere in this volume, and aim to emphasize new and innovative opportunities to change the way we think about and govern Canadian waters. Moreover, this chapter seeks to move past, but certainly not minimize the importance of, current water challenges in Canada by searching for "cracks" in current water policy frameworks where spaces for productive change can be carved out without changing our current water policies.

I would like to return to two questions posed earlier in this chapter. What are the governance opportunities for water and what opportunities or lessons can water create for governance? In terms of the former, the most salient point presented here relates to breaking down the widespread nature-society binary by integrating questions of water, human health, and ecosystem health in innovative and holistic ways. Since water is a flow resource that transcends the human-nature binary, there exists a tremendous opportunity here to find innovative governance solutions that recognize and address this constructed distinction. For example, the conscious integration of land and water resources might be one way to work through the nature/human binary. If zoning decisions were reviewed by municipal boards *and* water-related decision-making bodies, the process might force the two into conversation. Another way to integrate the two might be to cross-pollinate human resources between the two departments or ministries in order to help break down departmental silos and encourage more integration.

The second question about water opportunities for governance speaks to ways in which issues around water can be used as a vehicle for governance innovation more generally. The work in this chapter and, more broadly, in this book relates to the issue of breaking down silos. In Canada, silos exist between the natural and social sciences, between various levels of government, and between policy-makers and the public. These silos continue to hinder efforts to create more integrative policy. Water presents an ideal opportunity to break down artificial distinctions between departments and jurisdictions and it is our hope that taking advantage of such opportunities can build institutional bridges that might apply to other policy areas. Another way in which water could provide a source of governance innovation relates to the National Water Strategy discussed above. The journey toward a National Water policy can act as an opportunity for experimentation with different forms of innovative and collaborative governance. These new forms of innovation and collaboration could be applied to other facets of environmental governance in Canada.

Figure 1 of this chapter identifies two axes along which various water governance initiatives may be situated. Each of the opportunities presented in this chapter may fall in a different quadrant of that graph. In that spirit, I ask readers of this volume to think more broadly about the kinds of governance arrangements that they deem as productive or useful, to expand conventional colonial thinking of what constitutes "government-led" decision-making arrangements, and to question the relationships between particular governance arrangements and policy goals. The links between this section of the volume and discussions elsewhere regarding ethics, in particular, offer unique synergies for movement forward. I hope therefore to leave the reader not in despair for Canadian waters, but rather, hungry for innovation and empowered with new ideas.

References

Allan, A., and Wouters, P. 2004. *What Role for Water Law in the Emerging "Good Governance" Debate?*. Paper presented at the NATO Advanced Research Workshop, Bishkek, Kyrgyzstan, February 23-27.

Amos, B., Lammey, J., Cairns, M., and Turan, C. 2011. *Getting Tough on Environmental Crime? Holding the Government of Canada to Account on Environmental Enforcement.* Vancouver, BC: Ecojustice Canada.

Andrews, M. 2008. The Good Governance Agenda: Beyond Indicators without Theory. *Oxford Development Studies* 36(4): 379-407.

Bakker, K. 2003. *Good Governance in Restructuring Water Supply: A Handbook.* [Commissionned by the Federation of Canadian Municipalities and the Program on Water Issues] Ottawa, ON: Federation of Canadian Municipalities.

Bakker, K. 2007. *Commons or Commodity? The Debate over Private Sector Involvement in Water Supply.* In "Eau Canada," ed. Bakker, K. Vancouver and Toronto: UBC Press. Chp. 9.

Bakker, K., and Cook, C. 2011. Water Governance in Canada: Innovation and Fragmentation. *International Journal of Water Resources Development* 27(2): 275-89.

Batterbury, S. P., and Fernando, J. L. 2006. Rescaling Governance and the Impacts of Political and Environmental Decentralization: An Introduction. *World Development* 34(11): 1851-63.

Boyd, D. 2003. *Unnatural Law: Rethinking Canadian Environmental Law and Policy.* Vancouver, BC: UBC Press.

Braun, B., and Castree, N., eds. 2001. *Social Nature: Theory, Practice, and Politics.* Malden, MA: Wiley-Blackwell.

CBC News. 2011. *Attawapiskat Crisis Sparks Political Blame Game* CBC/Radio-Canada, http://www.cbc.ca/news/canada/story/2011/12/01/attawapiskat-thursday.html.

CEPI. 2011. *The Spirit of the Lakes Speaks. Bras D'or Lakes Collaborative Environmental Planning Initiative.* Available from http://brasdorcepi.ca/documents/reports/.

Christensen, R. 2011. *Waterproof 3: Canada's Drinking Water Report Card.* Vancouver/ Ottawa/Toronto/Calgary: Ecojustice Canada. Available from http://www.ecojustice. ca/reports-publications/research/.

Clarke, T. 2008. *Turning on Canada's Tap?: Why We Need a Pan-Canadian Policy and Strategy Now on Bulk Water Exports to the US:* Polaris Institute. Available from http://www. polarisinstitute.org/reports.

Cohen, A., and Harris, L. 2014. *Performing Scale: Watersheds as "Natural" Governance Units in the Canadian Context.* In "Performativity, Space, and Politics," eds. Rose-Redwood, R. and Glass, M. New York/Abingdon: Routledge.

Cook, C. L. *Putting the Pieces Together: Tracing Jurisdictional Fragmentation in Ontario Water Governance.* Ph.D. Thesis, University of British Columbia, 2011.

Cox, K. R. 1998. Spaces of Dependence, Spaces of Engagement and the Politics of Scale, Or: Looking for Local Politics. *Political Geography* 17(1): 1-23.

Doornbos, M. 2001. "Good Governance": The Rise and Decline of a Policy Metaphor? *Journal of Development Studies* 37(6): 93-108.

Dunn, G., and Bakker, K. 2011. Fresh Water-Related Indicators in Canada: An Inventory and Analysis. *Canadian Water Resources Journal* 36(2): 135-48.

Eggertson, L. 2008. Investigative Report: 1766 Boil-Water Advisories Now in Place across Canada. *Canadian Medical Association Journal* 178(10): 1261-63.

Environment Canada. 1987. *Federal Water Policy.* Government of Canada. Available from http://www.publications.gc.ca/pub?id=463942&sl=0.

European Commission. 2003. *Report from the Commission on European Governance.* Luxembourg: Office for Official Publications of the European Communities.

de Loë, R. 2008a. Invited Commentary: Canada Needs a National Water Strategy. *Canadian Water Resources Journal* 33(4): 309-14.

de Loë, R. 2008b. *Toward a Canadian National Water Strategy.* [Final Report prepared for the Canadian Water Resources Association]. Guelph, ON.

de Loë, R. 2009. A Canadian Vision and Strategy for Water in the 21st Century. *Policy Options* 30(7): 21-24.

Graham, J., Amos, B., and Plumptre, T. 2003. *Principles for Good Governance in the 21st Century. Policy Brief No.15.* Ottawa, ON: Institute on Governance.

Grindle, M. S. 2004. Good Enough Governance: Poverty Reduction and Reform in Developing Countries. *Governance* 17(4): 525-48.

Grindle, M. S. 2007. Good Enough Governance Revisited. *Development Policy Review* 25(5): 533-74.

Harrison, K. 1996. *Passing the Buck: Federalism and Canadian Environmental Policy*. Vancouver, BC: UBC Press.

Hill, C., Furlong, K., Bakker, K., and Cohen., A. 2008. Harmonization Versus Subsidiarity in Water Governance: A Review of Water Governance and Legislation in the Canadian Provinces and Territories. *Canadian Water Resources Journal* 33(4): 315-32.

Hill, C., and Harrison, K. 2006. *Intergovernmental Regulation and Municipal Drinking Water*. In "Rules, Rules, Rules, Rules: Multilevel Regulatory Governance," eds. Doern, G. B. and Johnson, R. Toronto, ON: University of Toronto Press.

Kettl, D. F. 2000. The Transformation of Governance: Globalization, Devolution, and the Role of Government. *Public Administration Review* 60(6): 488-97.

Lockwood, M. 2010. Good Governance for Terrestrial Protected Areas: A Framework, Principles and Performance Outcomes. *Journal of Environmental Management* 91(3): 754-66.

Morris, T. J., Boyd, D. R., Brandes, O. M., Bruce, J. P., Hudon, M., Lucas, B., Maas, T., Nowlan, L., Pentland, R., and Phare, M. 2007. *Changing the Flow: A Blueprint for Federal Action on Freshwater*: The Gordon Water Group of Concerned Scientists and Citizens.

NAFA. 2000. *Aboriginal Participation in Forest Management: Not Just Another Stakeholder*: National Aboriginal Forestry Association. Available from http://www.nafaforestry. org/publications.php.

Nanda, V. P. 2006. The "Good Governance" Concept Revisited. *Annals of the American Academy of Political and Social Science* 603(1): 269-83.

Norman, E. S. 2012. Cultural Politics and Transboundary Resource Governance in the Salish Sea. *Water Alternatives* 5(1): 138-60.

Nowlan, L., and Bakker, K. 2007. *Delegating Water Governance: Issues and Challenges in the BC Context*. Vancouver, BC: UBC Program on Water Governance.

Nowlan, L., and Bakker, K. 2010. *Practising Shared Water Governance in Canada: A Primer*. Vancouver, BC: UBC Program on Water Governance.

NRTEE. 2011. *Charting a Course: Sustainable Water Use by Canada's Natural Resource Sectors*. Ottawa, ON: National Round Table on the Environment and the Economy.

Paehlke, R. 2000. Environmentalism in One Country: Canadian Environmental Policy in an Era of Globalization. *Policy Studies Journal* 28(1): 160-75.

Peters, B. G., and Pierre, J. 1998. Governance without Government? Rethinking Public Administration. *Journal of Public Administration Research and Theory* 8(2): 223-43.

Quinn, F. 2007. *Water Diversion, Export and Canada-Us Relations: A Brief History*. Toronto, ON: Munk Centre for International Studies. Program on Water Issues.

Rhodes, R. A. W. 1996. The New Governance: Governing without Government. *Political Studies* 44(4): 652-67.

Rogers, P., and Hall, A. W. 2003. *Effective Water Governance* TEC Background Papers No. 7: Global Water Partnership.

Rose-Redwood, R. 2011. Rethinking the Agenda of Political Toponymy. *ACME: An International E-Journal for Critical Geographies* 10(1): 34-41.

Salamon, L. M., and Elliott, O. V. 2002. *The Tools of Government: A Guide to the New Governance*. Oxford, UK: Oxford University Press.

Scoffield, H. 2011. Locals Disagree on Who's to Blame for Attawapiskat Crisis. *The Globe and Mail*. http://www.theglobeandmail.com/news/national/locals-disagree-on-whos-to-blame-for-attawapiskat-crisis/article2254245/.

Standing Senate Committee on Energy, the Environment and Natural Resources. 2005. *Water in the West: Under Pressure*. Ottawa, ON: Senate of Canada.

Turton, A. R., Hattingh, J., Claassen, M., Roux, D. J., and Ashton, P. J. 2007. *Towards a Model for Ecosystem Governance: An Integrated Water Resource Management Example*. In "Governance as a Trialogue: Government-Society-Science in Transition," eds. Turton, A. R., Hattingh, J. H., Maree, G. A., Roux, D. J., Claassen, M. and Strydom, W. F. Berlin, Heidelberg: Springer Verlag Berlin Heidelberg. 1-28.

von der Porten, S., and de Loë, R. 2010. *Water Challenges and Solutions in First Nations Communities: Summary of Findings from the Workshop Sharing Water Challenges and Solutions: Experience of First Nations Communities, April 15-16, 2010, Kitchener-Waterloo, Ontario*. Water Policy and Governance Group.

Whatmore, S. 1999. *Hybrid Geographies: Rethinking the "Human" in Human Geography*. In "Human Geography Today," eds. Massey, D., Allen, J. and Sarre, P. Malden, MA: Blackwell. 22-40.

Legislation and Case Law

The Constitution Act, 1867 (UK), 30 & 31 Victoria, c 3.

Delgamuukw v. *British Columbia*, (1997) 3 S.C.R. 1010.

Changing Societal Values
Implications for Water Management and Social Opportunities

Henning Bjornlund, Ph.D.
Department of Economics, University of Lethbridge

Vibeke Bjornlund
Research Manager, University of Lethbridge

1. Introduction

Since the emergence of the first organized societies, land, water and other natural resources have been managed and used in pursuit of societal values, social opportunities and policy objectives of the time. In early days, these were defined by local rulers and were often linked to military objectives such as securing food for armies and the loyalty of their leaders, rewarding returning soldiers, encouraging the settlement and security of border regions, and increasing the taxation base to fund the armies (Bjornlund and Bjornlund 2013).

Since the industrial revolution, economic and population growth has been exponential, resulting in similar growth in resource extraction and intensification in the use of (among other resources) water, fish, wood, and land. Over the last two centuries, in places like Australia, Canada and the United States, water has been largely seen as a series of social opportunities: an incentive to settle remote regions, a means by which to produce energy and increase food production, and importantly a "free" waste disposal mechanism all factors which could drive economic activity in a rapidly industrializing society. Pursuing these social opportunities has had environmental consequences.

These consequences intensified after the Second World War; eventually the public awareness of environmental degradation of major water resources began to increase due to a series of events. In North America, two important examples include i) recurring incidents of dead fish washing ashore along the coast of Lake Erie in the early 1960s (Brand et al. 1988), and ii) the burning of the Cuyahoga

River in Cleveland, Ohio in 1969, due to contamination by chemical effluent (Adler 2002). The book Silent Spring by Rachel Carson (1962) also raised the awareness of the impact of chemicals on the natural environment and was instrumental in increasing public awareness of environmental issues.

By the late 1960s the magnitude and nature of resource use had reached unsustainable levels in many places, leading to serious resource depletion and degradation, and threatening the environment and the ecosystems on which people depend. Over time, it became clear that this level of resource use could not continue, and that new policies were needed in order to reverse serious environmental impacts. Such changes were observed across a range of resource-dependent sectors, such as the cod fisheries of Newfoundland and Labrador (Gissurarson 2000; Brubaker 2000). In this province, fishing peaked in the late 1950s, after which the population of cod declined and ultimately collapsed; prolonged debates resulted in a moratorium on the fishery in 1993 (Frank et al. 2005). Similarly, policies have been enacted to protect water resources in places around the world; for example, water extraction from the Ogallala Aquifer in the United States and the Murray River in Australia are now strictly controlled through policy (Guru and Horne 2000; Clark and Moore 1985). Overcoming the consequences of past policies has been a challenge for policy makers since the early 1970s. In responding to this challenge, new social opportunities that reflect the values and policy objectives of today's society may be found.

The next section of this chapter discusses elements of the new policy paradigm that have emerged since the early 1970s, and explores how changing social values toward water and other natural resources have driven this process. The third section describes the challenges associated with policy implementation focusing on water resources, specifically on the irrigation sector as it accounts for 80% of water use in the most stressed basins. The fourth section uses Alberta, Canada as a case study to explore how the implementation of these policies has been received. The final section provides a discussion of some social opportunities emerging from implementing the new policy paradigm.

2. Reversing the Trend from Expanding to Contracting Resource Use

Towards the end of the 1960s, the impact of ever-increasing resource extraction on the environment had become increasingly obvious. Television allowed the public to visualize many of these problems in a way that had been unavailable to past generations. Increased affluence, an abundance of recreational time, and use of the automobile brought a larger proportion of the population into direct and regular contact with the natural environment. As a result, society's values started to change, and the quality of water resources became a public issue.

When the conservation movement began in the 19th century, the focus was on wilderness preservation rather than true ecological conservation. The movement mainly attracted members of the more affluent part of the society, who wanted to preserve wilderness areas to secure their continued use for sport and recreation, including activities such as hunting. At that time, there was no evident conflict between conservation and economic growth. In the 1960s, however, the connections between economic growth, increasing pollution, and resource degradation started to become clear. The emerging environmental movement, driven by knowledge of these connections, subsequently challenged once-accepted values and entered the political arena (McCormick 1995).

In response to these changes in social values, a new policy paradigm began to emerge, primarily under the auspices of the United Nations. The Stockholm Declaration and Action Plan of 1972, followed by the report of the World Commission on the Environment and Development of 1987, were important milestones on the path to the Rio Declaration and Agenda 21 of 1992. Key elements of Agenda 21 as it applies to water are: i) public participation in water management; ii) devolution of decision making; iii) the legitimate right of the environment to water; iv) water as an economic good; v) pricing of water and other economic incentives; vi) more efficient and productive water use; and vii) integration of economic, social and environmental considerations (Sitarz 1993). These principles remain important, and are echoed in recent water policies introduced at the national and regional levels, such as the Alberta Water for Life strategy (AE 2003) and the Council of Australian Governments' Water Reform Agreements in Australia (CoAG1994, 2004).

Many of these policies reflect the seemingly "new" perception that water should be treated as an economic good, and that economic instruments should guide its allocation and use. While this perception was presented in the 1990s as a major shift in policy direction, economic instruments have been used to achieve policy objectives related to the use of natural resources for the last 5,000 years (Bjornlund and Bjornlund 2013). What is new is a change in what people are trying to achieve with these tools. Throughout history, economic instruments have been used to encourage resource users to behave in ways consistent with societies' objectives, primarily in terms of increasing resource extraction and intensifying their use. Thus, incentives have been provided to clear more land, extract more water, fell more trees, drain more land, or catch more fish. These are expansionary objectives, which most resource users and their communities align with, as they increase the opportunity to create economic activity, jobs and wealth. By comparison, recent changes have meant that economic instruments are being promoted to reduce resource use, which is far more problematic for resource users and their communities, but which also creates new social opportunities.

Private individuals and organizations can now use markets to achieve environmental goals by buying water or paying farmers to change their practices. Similarly, Governments can buy back irrigators' water and pay them to change land use practices to increase the provision of ecosystem services (Wheeler et al. 2013; Bjornlund 2004)

3. The Challenge of the New Direction – The Case of Water

In response to over-allocation of water and associated environmental degradation, many river basins, such as the South Saskatchewan River Basin (SSRB) in Alberta (AE 2005) and the Murray-Darling Basin in Australia have been "closed" – meaning that no new applications for licenses to extract water are being accepted. With continued population and economic growth, coupled with increased demand to reduce water extraction to sustainable levels, our societies are faced with at least four interrelated challenges: i) how to meet new demand from existing and new consumptive users; ii) how to provide more water to the environment; iii) how to deal with the socioeconomic impact of achieving the first two challenges; and iv) how to involve the public in the planning process. This section focuses on the first three challenges, while the last is discussed in Section 5.

Meeting demand for both consumers and the environment can be addressed in two ways: i) governments can use "command and control" or regulatory measures to reallocate water rights; or ii) mechanisms can be created to apply market measures to water use. Certainly the regulatory reallocation of water can be accomplished, with sufficient political will (Bjornlund 2010). This will is often lacking, however, and hence the preference for market solutions. An argument for regulatory reallocation of water is that the resource belongs to society, which gave license holders the privilege of putting it to use and in turn delivering benefit back to society. Now that society's interests have changed, however, water should be reallocated in accordance with today's social values. A counter-argument is that society has invested heavily in water infrastructure, providing water at little or no cost to irrigators in order to entice settlers to otherwise unattractive areas, ultimately increasing food production. In response, irrigators have invested their own money in putting the water to the use that corresponded with the social values of the time (food production), and that these investments will be largely lost if the water is taken away. In essence, regulatory reallocation asks irrigators to pay for the changes in social interests and values – is that fair?

This conflict has driven many jurisdictions to introduce market measures – securing water for the environment by buying water back from irrigators and other water users, as is currently done in Australia and the United States (Wheeler et al. 2013). However, valuing water is difficult; furthermore, the price set for water rights may indirectly dictate "how much" water should be reallocated to the environment. While there is generally strong agreement with the notion that the environment needs more water, there is far less agreement on how much water is needed, who should carry the burden of providing it, and what a fair price for the resource is (Whitford 2010; Bjornlund 2005; Bjornlund et al. 2011).

Changing access to water resources, either through regulatory means or via market forces, creates a new set of socio-economic challenges for resource users and their communities. If irrigators receive less water, it could reduce their income earning capacity and thereby the value of their assets. If irrigators' income earning capacity is reduced, then they will employ fewer people, spend less in local stores, make less use of local service providers, and pay less in property taxes (Fenton 2007; Edwards et al. 2008). At the community scale, this could lead to a reduction in local services available, potentially resulting in out migration. The degree of socioeconomic impact will in part depend upon the capacity of water users to increase efficiency and productivity of water use. If more commodities and income can be generated from a unit of water, then a reduction in water use might have little or no socioeconomic consequences – but how might this be achieved? Options include private initiatives and investments, direct government investment and economic incentives to private water users. One option would require water users to achieve a certain level of water use efficiency, as demonstrated in Arizona where limits were set for how much water can be used by each type of water user (Johnson and Caster 1999). For example, a mine in that state must recycle between 75-85% of all water used in order to reach the maximum water allocation. Maximum water use is also defined for all farms based on crop water use and the most efficient irrigation technologies. Such standards can be revised over time as water application and conveyance technologies are improved.

If limits are placed on water use, particularly on a per-product basis, it is important to know what happens to the water that is saved. If it simply accrues to the water user, as it does in many jurisdictions, then it is likely to be put to further economic use resulting in increased net use. Thus, while the user is being more efficient with water consumption on a per unit basis, the net effect is more product and less water for the environment and downstream users. On the other hand, if governments invest in improved efficiency or subsidize users to be more efficient, they may prefer to allocate the saved water to the environment. Either case presents different kinds of opportunities.

Socioeconomic impacts may also be mitigated by the manner in which cuts to water access are implemented. If irrigators are adequately compensated, it might assist them to make adjustments to manage with less water, i.e. improving water-use efficiency and productivity. If structural adjustment support is provided to communities, alternative jobs and income opportunities might be developed, which would help communities to retain population and remain viable. Facing these three challenges – providing water for society, for the environment, and managing socio-economic impacts – therefore also create opportunities for society to respond in ways that conserve water, protect the environment, and sustain socioeconomic activity.

4. Society's Response to the New Policy Direction – The Case of Alberta

Recent Policy Reforms in Alberta

Since the late 1990s, in partial response to Agenda 21, Alberta has introduced a number of new acts and policies. The *Water Act* 1999 and the *Irrigation District Act* 2000 introduced trading in licensed water allocations and public participation in water planning including identifying water conservation objectives. The Water for Life strategy (AE 2003) represents Alberta's long-term vision for how water should be used and the need for public private partnerships in water planning and management. This strategy acknowledges that a major shift needs to take place in the way water is managed and that future demand for water might exceed available supply. The strategy promotes the use of economic instruments, best management practices, improved water use efficiency and productivity, and public involvement in water planning processes as the main elements of securing future supply. It states that existing water licenses will be respected and reallocation will be on a voluntary basis, but emphasizes that economic instruments will be used as needed to secure the outcomes.

The urgency of policy reform was emphasized in the background paper to the draft South Saskatchewan River Basin (SSRB) Management Plan (AE 2005). It noted that 22 of 33 main river reaches suffer from moderate environmental impacts, five are heavily impacted and three are environmentally degraded as a consequence of the current level of water extraction. It also noted that demand from irrigators and non-irrigators will increase significantly over the next four decades. As a consequence, the SSRB, except for the Red Deer River, was closed to applications for new water licenses by the Government of Alberta in 2005 following the approval of the draft water management plan. This increased the need for mechanisms to share the water available under existing water licenses as well as reducing the current level of extraction.

In 2008 the Alberta Land Use Framework (LUF) was introduced, followed by the 2009 *Alberta Land Stewardship Act* (ALSA); these pieces of policy are critical in connecting land use actions with aquatic ecosystems and recognizing that the environment provides "public goods" that Albertans enjoy and value. ALSA is also critical as it has legal precedence over all other acts dealing with environment and natural resource management. Both LUF and ALSA support the use of market-based instruments, and for the first time list a number of instruments that can be used (Kerr and Bjornlund 2010). The documents also introduce the need for integrated resource management and planning and provide a governance structure for these processes involving new Regional Advisory Councils. While ALSA provides a strong integrated approach, the role of existing water management plans that have been or are in the process of being completed is unclear, and there is some evidence of dissatisfaction with constantly changing governance structures (Kerr and Bjornlund 2011).

Experiences with Water Sharing in Alberta

As discussed, the Alberta Government places great reliance on voluntary reallocations of water resources, and on water savings through improved water use efficiency, as mechanisms to meet new social demand as well as the needs of the environment. This approach has been in place for more than a decade, so it is possible to evaluate its success. The uptake of water trading among irrigators has been very slow, with five "arms-length" transactions recorded over the first five years (Nicol et al. 2008) and limited activity ever since. There was some activity in the market for "temporary trade" of water rights[1] during the 2001 drought, which played an important role in allowing irrigators to manage that challenge (Nicol and Klein 2006).

A survey of managers and board members across the 13 irrigation districts found that only 24% supported the use of any kind of economic instruments, with 8% agreeing with the right to transfer licensed allocations, 15% with water assignment and 21% with subsidizing producers to improve water use efficiency and productivity (Bjornlund et al. 2007). The survey also revealed that only 26% agreed that water saved through such improvements should go to the environment while 69% agreed that it should be used to bring more dry land under irrigation (Bjornlund et al. 2008).

The first attempt of a major water transfer from irrigation to municipal use was made in 2007 when a developer proposed a major shopping mall, casino and race track at Balzac (north of Calgary). The Calgary water authority refused to

---

[1] An assignment under the Water Act, 1999 give the owner of a licensed water allocation the opportunity to assign all or part of their available water under their license to another license holder. This is in some jurisdiction referred to as trading in the temporary right to use water or for short "temporary trading."

supply the water as the development was outside their territory. The developer then attempted to obtain the Water from the Red Deer River, where new licenses are still being issued. The development was outside the Red Deer basin, however, and delivering water to it would require an inter-basin transfer, which requires approval by the Minister in charge. In this case, such an approval was not forthcoming. Finally, a deal was struck with the Western Irrigation District (WID) to transfer 2.5 billion litres of its licence to the development. The developer would pay C\$15 million for the water rights, cash which the WID would use to replace a leaky canal with a pipeline – an improvement that would save more water than sold through the deal. This transfer represents a win-win situation, allowing significant economic development and generating both a financial gain and access to more water for the WID. Under the Irrigation District Act such a transfer needs to be approved by a majority of irrigators in a plebiscite; it was only approved by a narrow margin and attracted significant public controversy and opposition from irrigators, environmental NGOs, water and electricity authorities and other special interest groups, resulting in court cases (Christensen and Droitsch 2008). The transfer was finally approved in 2007 and the shopping mall has been constructed.

The example above illustrates the low level of public support for water trading. In response, irrigation districts have attempted to find other ways of sharing their excess water with other users without relinquishing their water licenses. Under the Water Act it is possible for irrigation districts to enter into supply agreements with other water users (such as municipalities) if their license allows it. In 2007, the Eastern Irrigation District applied to have its license amended to supply water for non-irrigation purposes in order to meet growing demands from surrounding communities and industries. Similar amendments had been made to licenses in the past, although some argued that the ability of the districts to effectively determine who got the right to use water at what price undermined the strong public interest in water laid down in the 1999 Water Act (Bankes and Kwasniak 2005). In this particular case, environmental lobby groups effectively opposed the amendment (Christensen and Droitsch 2008) causing Alberta Environment to stop processing the application pending further investigation. The argument against the amendment was that it would allow the district to provide water to any user willing to pay, essentially created a mechanism of circumventing the environmental assessments required for the formal transfer of a water licence. When the amendment was approved (18 November 2010), it was appealed (17 December 2010) by Ecojustice and others. The final appeal was dismissed as of 18 October 2012 (Alberta EAB 2012).

Despite the fact that both of these cases are clearly in line with the spirit of the Government's water strategy, and that it has been accepted by both scholars

and policymakers that water must be reallocated to align with society's changing needs and values (Baron et al. 2002; Alberta Environment 2008; Bjornlund
2010), it is clear that the method by which water resources are reallocated is still
subject to debate (Brewer et al. 2008). In particular, the use of markets for reallo-
cating water is seen as problematic by some environmentalists (Christensen and
Droitsch 2008), a feeling which has gained significant support within the wider
community (Percy 2005; Brewer et al. 2008).

5. Social Opportunities in the Process of Change

Meeting new demand from existing and new consumptive users, while also
providing more water to the environment, and managing the socioeconomic
impact of achieving these goals requires radical reforms and new and innovative
solutions. Implementing radical reforms provides opportunities for fresh
thinking and significant changes in direction; herein lies the opportunity for
incorporating the changing social values and identifying and achieving new
social opportunities.

Public participation in water management clearly provides opportunities for
stakeholders and local communities to get involved in, and have a say in, how
water resources should be managed, defining the need of the environment and
having a say in how water should be shared between competing users. Such an
involvement helps to ensure that the changing community values are reflected
in water management decisions; it can also build social capital for the continued
adaptive management of water resources. Social capital is going to be increasingly important in adaptive water management processes, as climate change is
likely to strain water resources and create more and longer instances of water
scarcity in the future. Social capital built through an adaptive process could also
support other community-based activities. Other chapters in this volume provide excellent examples of how local engagement around water resources have
provided opportunities to implement change of great social benefit and importance. Research indicates that involvement in such processes positively influ-
ences peoples' perception of the environment, and increases their willingness to
implement policies to protect the environment while considering the impact of
current water users and their communities (Bjornlund et al. 2011and 2012; Russenberger et al. 2011a, b)

Water markets provide an opportunity for governments, non-government organizations (NGOs) and individuals to take action to protect their environmental and social interest by buying water and/or paying farmers to change their
management practices to provide ecosystem services to further improve environmental outcome and recreational and lifestyle benefits (Bjornlund 2004). In

places like the United States and Australia this has taken place to quite some extent (Garrick et al. 2009 and 2011; Wheeler et al. 2013). Under the right governance structure, it is possible that organizations of anglers and whitewater rafters would be willing to buy water to augment river flow to improve their recreational value of a stream. This is not currently possible in jurisdictions like Alberta, however, as only the Government can hold water for in-stream use. It has been argued that this limitation in the Water Act should be reworked (Kwasniak 2010; Bjornlund 2010). One area of concern is that if private individuals and NGOs are allowed to hold in-stream licenses they can apply for licenses on rivers which are not currently closed and thereby block future development (pers. com. Dave McGee). This could be avoided, however, by restricting the ability of NGOs and individuals to only hold licenses that they have purchased in the market. Once conservation objectives have been defined for all rivers through planning processes involving all key stakeholders, it could be argued that minimum levels of environmental flows acceptable to the broader society have been satisfied. It could then be left to special interest groups to augment this flow to meet their specific objectives via the market using their own funds. A recent survey of households in Southern Alberta indicated that about 45% agree with such a policy, while only about 30% disagree suggesting that it would not be viable to introduce it (Bjornlund et al. 2012).

Conclusions

Water and other natural resources have for many thousands of years been used to pursue socio-economic opportunities. The post-Second World War period started to see some of the environmental consequences of achieving these objectives, and public opinion started to change. The 1970s saw the emergence of a new policy paradigm designed to reverse the trend of environmental degradation. New policies emerged during this period aimed at reducing resource extraction, and at designing resource use to minimize environmental damage. We have argued that this policy paradigm includes two main elements which open up opportunities for members of the society to have at least a say in which social opportunities should be prioritized when deciding how scarce resources should be used.

The need for public participation in the decision making process with respect to water planning and management opens up one field of opportunity. In Alberta, for example, key stakeholder groups are invited to participate mainly by providing advice to the Minister of the Environment. This allows individuals and stakeholder groups to at least have a say in the process. It also facilitates social capacity building and raises the awareness of water issues in the general popu-

 Changing Societal Values

lation, which will strengthen the public influence in future resource planning and can have an effect on other social issues.

The use of markets to reallocate scarce water resources also enables individual and key special interest groups to acquire water in the market to meet their own specific social objectives, to pool their resources and make a difference. For example groups of anglers or white water rafters could buy water to increase water flow or water quality to improve rivers or stretches of rivers for their specific purpose. Environmental groups could also buy water or pay farmers to change their management practices to improve water quality or the flow of rivers to better facilitate spawning of fish or survival of species. Similarly, governments could enter the market to buy-back water licenses to increase water flow. Such buy-back could be combined with additional payment to farmers to make management changes on their now dry land to improve the provision of ecosystem services to better reflect society values.

In the context of Alberta, the Water Act (1999) does not allow private individuals or non-government organizations to hold water licenses for in-stream purposes, as licenses are only granted for extractive purposes. It is argued that this should be changes to allow individual and non-government organizations to acquire water licenses for in-stream purposes.

One thing is certain: how we deal with water scarcity and associated environmental issues is one of the most challenging issues for many societies. To facilitate the necessary change to secure long-term environmental and social sustainability in water scarce regions, radical and innovative reforms are needed. Whenever such radical reforms take place there are also opportunities to change environmental and social objectives, to better reflect the needs and values of today's society.

References

Adler, J. 2002. Fables of the Cuyahoga: Reconstructing a History of Environmental Protection. *Fordham Environmental Law Journal* 14(1): 89-146.

Alberta Environment (AE). 2003. *Water for Life: Alberta's Strategy for Sustainability.* Edmonton, AB: Alberta Environment and Sustainable Resource Development. Available from http://www.waterforlife.alberta.ca/02488.html.

Alberta Environment (AE). 2005. *Background Information for Public Consultation on the South Saskatchewan River Basin Draft Water Management Plan.* Calcagy, AB: Alberta Environment.

Alberta Environment (AE). 2008. *Water for Life: A Renewal*. Edmonton, AB: Alberta Environment and Sustainable Resource Development. Available from http://www.waterforlife.alberta.ca/02488.html.

Alberta Environmental Appeals Board (EAB). 2012. *Honloch v. Director, Southern Region, Environmental Management, Alberta Environment and Sustainable Resource Development, re: Eastern Irrigation District* (18 October 2012), Appeal No. 10-043-R (A.E.A.B.).

Bankes, N., and Kwasniak, A. J. 2005. The St. Mary's Irrigation District License Amendment Decision: Irrigation Districts as a Law Unto Themselves. *Journal of Environmental Law and Practice* 16(1): 1-18.

Baron, J. S., Poff, N. L., Angermeier, P. L., Dahm, C. N., Gleick, P. H., Hairston Jr., N. G., Jackson, R. B., Johnston, C. A., Richter, B. D., and Steinman, A. D. 2002. Meeting Ecological and Societal Needs for Freshwater. *Ecological Applications* 12(5): 1247-60.

Bjornlund, H. 2004. Half a Billion Dollars – What About a Water Bank. *Water* 31(5): 18-19.

Bjornlund, H. 2005. Irrigators and the New Policy Paradigm – an Australian Case Study. *Water Policy* 7(6): 581-96.

Bjornlund, H. 2010. The Competition for Water: Striking a Balance among Social, Environmental, and Economic Needs. *C.D. Howe Institute Commentary* (302): 1-28.

Bjornlund, H., Nicol, L., and Klein, K. 2008. Implementing Alberta's Water for Life Strategy: An Irrigation Industry Perspective. *Praire Forum* 33(1): 167-90.

Bjornlund, H., Nicol, L., and Klein, K. 2007. Challenges in Implementing Economic Instruments to Manage Irrigation Water on Farms in Southern Alberta. *Journal of Agricultural Water Management* 92(3): 131-41.

Bjornlund, H., Parrack, C., and de Loë, R. 2013. Segmenting the Urban and Rural Populations of Southern Alberta for Improved Understanding of Policy Preferences for Water Reallocation. *Society & Natural Resources: An International Journal* 26(11): 1330-50.

Bjornlund, H., Xu, W., Zuo, A., and Wheeler, S. 2012. *Resource Dependence and Water Scarcity – How Do They Influence Policy Preferences for Water Sharing?* . Paper presented at the Conference of the International Water Resources Economics Consortium, part of the World Water Week, Stockholm, 26-31.

Bjornlund, H., Zuo, A., Parrack, C., Wheeler, S., and de Loë, R. 2011. *Water Reallocation Policies: Public Perceptions*. In "Water Resources Management VI," eds. Brebbia, C. A. and Popov, V. Southampton, UK: WITPress. 585-96.

Bjornlund, V., and Bjornlund, H. 2013. Economic Incentives: Successful in Expansion, Will It Also Be Successful in Contraction, . *International Journal of Sustainable Development and Planning* 8(3): 422-40.

Brand, C. J., Schmitt, S. M., Duncan, R. M., and Cooley, T. M. 1988. An Outbreak of Type E Botulism among Common Loons (Gavia Immer) in Michigan's Upper Peninsula. *Journal of Wildlife Diseases* 24(3): 471-76.

Brewer, J., Glennon, R., Ker, A., and Libecap, G. 2008. 2006 Presidential Address. Water Markets in the West: Prices, Trading, and Contractual Forms. *Economic Inquiry* 46(2): 91-112.

Brubaker, E. 2000. *Unnatural Disaster: How Politics Destroyed Canada's Atlantic Ground-fisheries.* In "Political Environmentalism: Going Behind the Green Curtain," ed. Anderson, T. L. Standford, CA: Hoover Institution Press. 161-210.

Carson, R. 1962. *Silent Spring.* Boston, MA: Houghton Mifflin.

Christensen, R., and Droitsch, D. 2008. *Fight to the Last Drop: A Glimpse into Alberta's Water Future.* Vancouver, BC: Ecojustice and Bow Riverkeeper.

Clark, S.D. and Moore, H. 1985. *Economic Criteria for Water Resource Planning and Management: Some Legal Implications.* In "Conservation and the Economy, Conference Papers and Proceedings," Canberra, Australia: Department of Arts, Heritage and the Environment, AGPS. 469-497.

Council of Australian Governments (CoAG). 1994. *Communiqué Meeting of CoAG, Hobart, Tasmania, February 25.* Available from http://www.pm.gov.au.

Council of Australian Governments (CoAG). 2004. *Communiqué Meeting of CoAG, Canberra, June 25.* Available from: http://www.pm.gov.au.

Edwards, J., Cheers, B., and Bjornlund, H. 2008. Social, Economic and Community Impacts of Water Markets in Australia's Murray Darling Basin Region. *International Journal of Interdisciplinary Social Sciences* 2(6): 1-10.

Fenton, M. 2007. *A Survey of Beliefs About Permanent Water Trading and Community Involvement in NRM in the Loddon Campaspe Irrigation Region of Northern Victoria.* [Report prepared for the North Central Catchment Management Authority and the Department of Primary Industries] Melbourne, Victoria.

Frank, K. T., Petrie, B., Choi, J. S., and Leggett, W. C. 2005. Trophic Cascades in a Formerly Cod-Dominated Ecosystem. *Science* 308(5728): 1621-23.

Garrick, D., Lane-Miller, C., and McCoy, A. 2011. Institutional Innovations for Governing Environmental Water in the Western U.S.: Lessons for Australia's Murray Darling-Basin. *Economic Papers* 30(2): 167-84.

Garrick, D., Siebentritt, M. A., Aylward, B., Bauer, C. J., and Purkey, A. 2009. Water Markets and Freshwater Ecosystem Services. *Ecological Economics* 69(2): 366-79.

Gissurarson, H. 2000. *Overfishing: The Icelandic Solution*. London, UK: Institute of Economic Affairs.

Guru, M., and Horne, J. 2000. *The Ogallala Aquifer*. Poteau, OK: The Kerr Center for Sustainable Agriculture.

Johnson, J. W., and Caster, L. J. 1999. *Tradability of Water Rights: Experiences of the Western United States*. In "Issues in Water Law Reform (Fao Legislative Study 67)," ed. FAO. Rome, Italy: Food and Agriculture Organization of the United Nations. 151-80.

Kerr, G. L., and Bjornlund, H. 2010. *Alberta's Drive to Use Market-Based Instruments for Ecosystem Services Provision*. In "Sustainable Irrication Management, Technologies and Policies III," eds. Brebbia, C. A., Marinov, A. M. and Bjornlund, H. Southampton, UK: WIT Press. 215-26.

Kerr, G. L., and Bjornlund, H. 2011. *Understanding the Acceptance of Market-Based Instruments for the Ecosystem Service of Water Quality*. In "Water and Society," eds. Pepper, W. D. and Brebbia, C. A. Southampton, UK: WITPress. 173-84.

Kwasniak, A. J. 2010. Water Scarcity and Aquatic Sustainability: Beyond Policy Limitations. *University of Denver Water Law Review* 13(2): 321-60.

McCormick, J. 1995. *The Global Environmental Movement*. London: John Wiley.

McGee, D., Director, Prairie Region, Natural Resources Service, Alberta Environment. Personal e-mail Communication, Noverber 21 2011.

Nicol L., and Klein, K. 2006. Water Market Characteristics: Results from a Survey of Southern Alberta Irrigators. *Canadian Water Resources Journal* 31(2): 91-104.

Nicol, L., Klein, K., and Bjornlund, H. 2008. Permanent Transfers of Water Rights: A Study of the Southern Alberta Market. *Praire Forum* 33(2): 341-56.

Percy, D. R. 2005. Responding to Water Scarcity in Western Canada. *Texas Law Review* 83(7): 2091-207.

Russenberger, M., Bjornlund, H., and Xu, W. 2011a. *Exploring Links between Policy Preferences for Water Reallocation and Beliefs, Values, Attitudes and Social Norms in Alberta, Canada*. In "Water and Society," eds. Pepper, W. D. and Brebbia, C. A. Southampton, UK: WITPress. 107-18.

Russenberger, M., Bjornlund, H., and Xu, W. 2011b. *Exploring Links between Policy Preferences for Water Reallocation and Beliefs, Values, Attitudes and Social Norms in Alberta, Canada*. Paper presented at the XIVth IWRA World Water Congress, Ipojuca, Brazil, September 25-29.

Sitarz, D., ed. 1993. *Agenda 21: The Earth Summit Strategy to Save Our Planet* Colorado: Earth Press.

Wheeler, S., Garrick, D., Loch, A., and Bjornlund, H. 2013. Evaluating Alternative Water Market Products to Acquire Water for the Environment in Australia. *Land Use Policy* 30(1): 427-36.

Whitford, T. 2010. *A Wider View of History Is Required to Understand the Murray Darling Basin*: Australian Policy and History. Available from www.aph.org.au/files/articles/widerView.htm.

Reconsidering Recent Trends in Municipal Governance
Lessons from Water Supply in Ontario, Canada[1]

Kathryn Furlong

Assistant Professor, Canada Research Chair in Urban Water Governance and Public Services, University of Montreal

This chapter is concerned with municipal governance in the context of recent trends to make municipalities more "cost-efficient" while reducing their influence over service delivery. The example of water supply is used to explore the opportunity for municipal governments to reassert their role in service delivery and to ask what is needed to enable municipalities to meet their wide-ranging and challenging mandates. Although this chapter focuses on the particular case of Ontario, Canada, the reforms and challenges discussed are applicable to a variety of jurisdictions, especially in North America.

Throughout the 1980s and the 1990s, the roles of local governments in service provision, and of senior governments in regulation, were challenged across a variety of contexts. At the municipal scale, it was argued that services should be made independent from local government. This was to be done through organizational reforms such as privatization and alternative service delivery (ASD), the latter of which involves service models that are at arm's length from local government (see Furlong and Bakker 2010). At higher scales, the regulatory role of senior governments was initially "rolled back." However, the need for senior government regulation across a variety of issue areas, including water supply, has since been reasserted (Levi-Faur 2005) and is now widely accepted even by its former critics (e.g. Trémolet and Halpern 2006; Water and Sanitation Program 2011). As Bakker argues, neoliberalism did not involve deregulation, so much as "re-regulation" (Bakker 2004).

---

[1] Some of the material has been published in Environment and Planning A as: Furlong, K., 2012. Good water governance without good urban governance? Regulation, service delivery models, and local government. Environment and Planning A 44 (11), 2721-2741

Water supply regulation is now accepted and promoted. Yet, the perceived need to delineate the role of municipal governments endures (e.g. Gassner et al. 2009). It is this continued questioning of the municipal role in service delivery that is the focus of this chapter. In Ontario, the drive to limit that municipal role is generally based on the premise that local councils tend to interfere with service delivery by impeding price increases, while simultaneously redirecting money reserved for water supply to other, more visible, municipal projects. Such issues, broadly characterized as the "politicization" of water supply, are widely cited as reasons for promoting organizational models that are independent from local government (e.g. Lee and Jouravlev 1997; Lee 1999). However, these issues rarely get fully discussed and in fact underscore the need to improve, rather than sideline, municipal governance.

The case of water supply reform in Ontario is examined in this chapter as an opportunity to contextualize the challenges of municipal governance in relation to service delivery. The key question that is asked is whether or not it is sufficient to restrict the influence of municipal governments over water supply (e.g. through privatization or ASD) in order to meet the challenges facing service delivery. Through the case study, it is argued that municipalities require the capacity (budgetary and authoritative) to fulfill their responsibilities in all service areas for water supply, even where senior government regulation has been strengthened, in order to enjoy long-term economic and environmental sustainability.

This chapter comprises three sections. In the first, I explore the literature on the role of senior and local governments in water supply. In section two, I present a case study of water supply in Ontario that is divided into four subsections. The first subsection begins with an examination of the underlying issues that have fostered the idea that local government influence over water supply should be minimized. In the second and third subsections, I discuss the promotion of arm's length service delivery models as the solution to these issues, as well as how these models have been affected by the strengthening of water supply regulation in the province. In the final subsection I explore why the role of municipal governments in service delivery remains important despite ASD and regulatory strengthening. The concluding section considers how water supply provides a social opportunity to reengage in holistic as opposed to segmented approaches to municipal governance. These discussions are based on research conducted between 2005 and 2007.[2]

---

[2] This research was conducted over an eight-month period between 2005 and 2006. It began with a survey in the spring of 2005. The survey data was used to draw out key themes in preparation for the case studies and is not presented here. Case studies were selected to represent transitions, completed or attempted, to an array of newly

Recent Trends Affecting Water Governance

Toward the end of the 1970s it became increasingly apparent that there were significant problems with respect to water supply across a range of contexts. In the Global North, water supplies suffered from underinvestment, limited wastewater treatment, and high levels of leakage and consumption (e.g. Kaïka 2005; Gandy 2002; Juuti and Katko 2005). Across a range of contexts, "state failure" was presented as a ready and generalized explanation for these challenges (e.g. Parker and Kirkpatrick 2005; Winpenny 1994). "State failure" can be defined as the inefficiency and ineffectiveness of the state in providing certain goods, like environmental protection (Jänicke 1990). The problem, it was argued, lay with phenomena such as "regulatory capture," whereby the government's role as both regulator and service provider enabled it to weaken oversight to its benefit (e.g. Lee and Jouravlev 1997; Anderson and Leal 2001). It was reasoned that local government should guide, but not manage, service delivery; it should "steer" and not "row" (Osborne and Gaebler 1992).

The proposed response to "state failure" involved the removal of the state from a variety of roles in favor of market-led governance and private sector service delivery. Following this logic, it was argued that water governance would improve through the use of market-based, full cost pricing and that the use of such pricing would result in water efficiency, appropriate allocation, and sustainable utilities (Anderson and Leal 1988; Lee 1999). The development of markets coupled with private sector discipline was predicted to reduce costs while increasing investment, transparency and efficiency (Lee and Jouravlev 1997). In this arrangement, the roles of senior and municipal governments were targeted in terms of the supposed negative effects of regulation on the part of the former and the politicization of service delivery on the part of the latter.

One way in which this took place was re-scaling. Broadly speaking, re-scaling involves the shifting of authority to higher scales combined with the shifting of responsibility to the municipal scale (Rhodes 1997; Brenner 2004; Jessop 2002). In general, such transfers of responsibility lack a corresponding shift in capacity, entitlements, and legitimacy to the municipal scale (Raco and Imrie 2000; Raco

---

adopted ASD models. They involved archival data collection and semi-structured key informant interviews with municipal staff, utility officials, municipal councilors, union representatives, conservation authorities and environmental groups. The research was followed by an expert workshop in April 2007, to discuss preliminary findings. There were 82 responses to the survey, fifty-three interviews, and 38 participants at the workshop. Due to research ethics requirements, the informants cannot be identified in a way that would enable an informed reader to ascertain their identity.

and Flint 2001). Municipal governments, in other words, are to "do more with less." In a variety of jurisdictions, affected municipalities tended to find their capacities to govern and provide services financially weakened, their policy flexibility reduced and their roles in service provision challenged (Jessop 2002). Rather than becoming effective in "steering" policy, in many instances this supposed role proved ill suited to the realities of local government (Hansen 2001).

Ironically, these types of reforms to environmental and municipal governance would later pave the way for a certain amount of state regulation to come back into the water sector across a range of contexts, from the UK to Ontario. Research has argued that deregulation is often followed by reregulation in order to consolidate state power and to establish the rules for the market-led management of natural resources (see Bakker 2000; MacLeod and Goodwin 1999). In several instances, senior governments also sought new regulation in order to limit the most damaging consequences of earlier reforms (Furlong 2010). Examples include measures to protect consumers (e.g. price caps, water quality requirements) and the environment (e.g. source water protection) (e.g. Bakker 2004; Hassan 1998; Snider 2004).

For many authors, the reassertion of senior government regulation solves the problem of service delivery models and the involvement of local governments. It is argued that the organizational model should not matter if the rules of the game are consistent, clear, sufficient, and enforced (i.e. if the institutions work) (see Budds and McGranahan 2003; Bakker et al. 2008). Even where organizational reforms involving private sector participation (PSP) are deemed problematic because of weak institutions (e.g. Castro 2007), it is the institutions, rather than service delivery models or the relationship between the two that remain central to analyses. In terms of organizational reforms for water supply, options that involve PSP have received the greatest attention. Alternative service delivery (ASD) includes options along a continuum from low to high independence from government (Fyfe 2004; Wilkins 2005). As such, most of the options are for public ownership and management and embody greater independence from municipal council than the municipal department model (e.g. public utilities commissions, municipal corporations, and community management).[3]

---

[3] For a detailed discussion of ASD, see Bakker and Cameron (2002) and Furlong and Bakker (2010).

An Example from Ontario

The Underlying Issues: Challenges Facing Municipalities

In Ontario, policy reform aimed at reducing government influence is largely associated with the Government of Premier Mike Harris and its *Common Sense Revolution* (1995-2002). The Harris government's associated policies, which focused on "doing more with less," had far-reaching impacts on both municipalities and environmental governance (Keil 2002; Walkom 1997). At the provincial scale, during the 1990s, environmental regulation and oversight were rolled-back (Montgomery 2002; Prudham 2004). For municipalities, the devolution of responsibilities from the provincial scale combined with forced budget cutting created important governance challenges (Keil 2002; Kipfer and Keil 2002; Downey and Williams 1998). Along with municipal amalgamations and the restructuring of the energy sector, these challenges drove ASD reform of municipal water departments (Furlong and Bakker 2011).

These policies, especially those related to environmental oversight, were heavily implicated in a water quality disaster in the town of Walkerton in June 2000 (O'Connor 2002; Prudham 2004) where seven people died and more than 1000 were made ill from consuming contaminated drinking water. However, even prior to the election of the Harris Government water supply in Ontario had been facing a series of issues. These issues included: low levels of investment in infrastructure, low levels of cost recovery, poor water use efficiency and insufficient source water protection (Christensen 2001; AMO, MEA, and OGRA 2001; Benidickson 2002). With the Walkerton Inquiry it would become apparent that there were also longstanding problems with employee qualification and oversight, especially in rural areas (O'Connor 2002).

The politicization of water supply by local councils was presented as a root cause of the above range of problems facing water supply in the province. In precisely the manner described above, municipal councils were said to prevent water departments from raising water rates and to use water funds to supplement the property tax (Martin et al. 2002; Swain et al. 2005). These tendencies were acknowledged by councilors, city staff, and utility managers interviewed for this research. For water supply, recovering costs is a problem of politics as well as one of economic planning. Politically, it can be difficult to raise water rates and to retain water revenue given insufficient accountability for full cost recovery and ring-fencing. Ring-fencing refers to the isolation of water budgets from municipal budgets such that water revenues and reserves cannot be applied to other municipal projects. Prior to Walkerton, municipalities tended to inhibit utilities from raising rates, as utility rates are one of the few visible costs to local constituents. However, exacerbated by their own limited revenue sources, municipal governments often sought to transfer limited water revenues and reserves to fund other municipal projects.[4]

In response to these issues, the separation of water utilities from direct municipal oversight was widely advocated. However, it is important to ask why municipal governments would "raid water reserves" (i.e. use water revenues and reserves to fund other projects). This research found three long-term challenges to water supply governance that have been particularly important. These include: the weak position of municipalities vis-à-vis higher scales of government, inadequate mechanisms for funding municipal services and insufficient accountability for water governance. These issues are already well documented in the literature (Keil 2002; Siegel 1997; Bird and Tassonyi 2001; McMillan 1997; Boyd 2003; de Loë and Kreutzwiser 2007). In the interests of space, I simply provide examples from the research that are demonstrative of these issues in Table 1.

Table 1: Long-term Challenges to Water Supply Governance in Ontario

Key Issue	Inter-scalar governance	Municipal funding	Accountability for water
Examples from this study	In 2002, Toronto approved a Special Committee of Council for Water and Wastewater to adhere to new regulations after Walkerton (e.g. for equipment and skilled personnel). Six-months later, it was rescinded as increasing the procurement abilities of any committee would require an amendment to the *Municipal Act* (Chief Administrative Officer 2002).	In an interview, a counselor in Peterborough highlighted the political difficulty of raising property taxes and the consequent need for new revenue sources such as a tourist tax.	Municipal water managers consistently identified the use of water revenues for other municipal projects as a key issue. The lack of accountability for ring-fencing and for utility performance on issues such as infrastructure maintenance made it possible to delay investments and to use the funds for other municipal projects.

Source: Compiled by the author.

---

[4] The issues discussed in this paragraph were cited in interviews with a senior federal bureaucrat (2006) and municipal councilors and utility management from four municipalities in 2005 and 2006.

The long-term challenges mentioned above were influenced by policy reform under the Harris government.[5] Among their first major reforms was the passage of the *Savings and Restructuring Act, (R.S.O. 1996, c.1)* which included changes to the *Municipal Act (see Savings and Restructuring Act, (R.S.O. 1996, c.1 s. M))* that were meant to promote municipal amalgamations and annexations. Another key piece of legislation, the *Services Improvement Act, (R.S.O. 1997, b.157)*, served to transfer a range of functions to municipalities from the province, including emergency services, sewage system inspections, boards of health, and social housing. Coupled with this increase in responsibilities, upon their election, the Harris government announced a 40% funding cut to municipalities within two years, amounting to a 16% decrease in municipal budgets (Siegel 1997).

Capital funding for infrastructure was also reduced. In 1999, the government established the Ontario SuperBuild Corporation as a single fund for all of the province's capital assets. According to Montgomery, this "was actually a massive reduction in provincial capital expenditure by more than half over five years" (Montgomery 2002, 212). This statement is supported by provincial data, collected for this project, which shows a sharp drop in Ontario infrastructure grants to municipalities, from 26% of total capital fund revenue in 1998 to 5% in 1999 (Figure 1, line: "Ontario Grants"). The Association of Municipalities of Ontario argued that the total realignment of funding and responsibilities yielded a $3 billion fiscal imbalance between the two scales of government (AMO 2005). The cuts to municipalities and infrastructure increased the pressure on the property tax and thus on the ability of municipalities to provide services (Tindal and Tindal 2004). It also significantly increased the pressure on municipal revenue and reserve funds, the contribution of which rose from 50% to 72% between 1997 and 1999 (see Figure 1, line: "Transfers from own sources").

These policies combined with two key pieces of legislation, the *Municipal Water and Sewerage Transfer Act, (R.S.O. 1997, c.6)* and the *Electricity Act (R.S.O. 1998, c.15)*. Both of these Acts served to heighten funding issues for water supply managers in particular. Through the former, the province transferred the ownership of 25% of existing water and sewage treatment plants to municipalities (230 in total) (SuperBuild 2002). In some cases, the transfer of ownership meant an increase in the municipal debt because the infrastructure deficit was now carried on the municipal ledger. The increase in debt load diminished municipal borrowing capacity as well as that of water utilities since they could not borrow independently. Taken together, these changes served to reinforce the

---

[5] The policy changes under the Harris government have been treated extensively elsewhere (e.g. Trebilcock and Hrab 2005) Here, I concentrate on the policies that proved central to water governance in the province.

long-term conflicts between municipalities and water governance discussed in Table 1. Through the *Electricity Act, (R.S.O. 1998, c.15)* municipalities were forced to separate all of the activities associated with their energy utilities, including equipment, and personnel. The result was to eliminate many of the economies of scale formerly achieved through sharing resources among utility services (i.e. water and energy in most cases). Consequently, many of the financial challenges facing municipalities and water utilities before these reforms were exacerbated.

Figure 1: Municipal Revenue Breakdown for Ontario 1977-2008

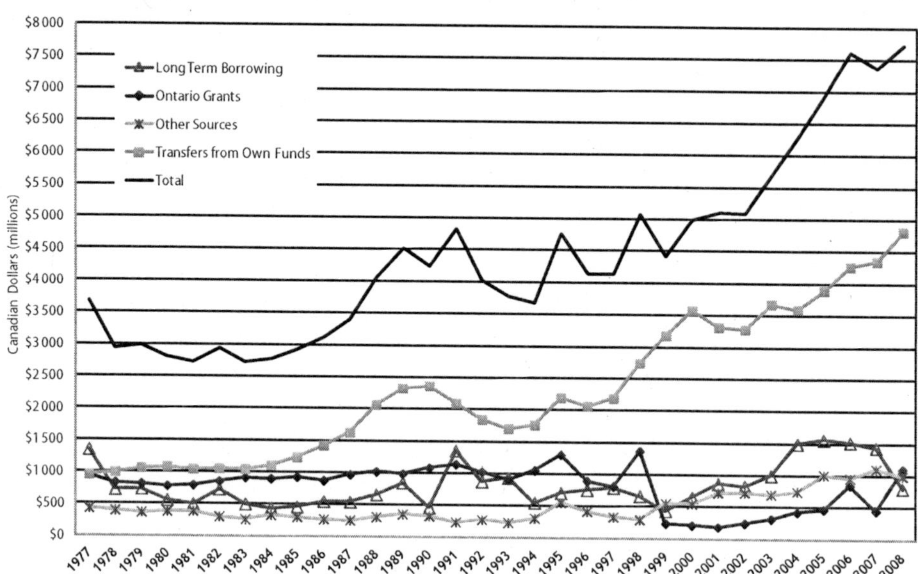

Source: Data from 1977-1999 made available upon request by the Ministry of Municipal Affairs and Housing (MMAH), Toronto, ON, data from 2000-2008 compiled from the MMAH Financial Information website (http://oraweb.mah.gov.on.ca/fir/). The data was corrected for inflation using Bank of Canada CPI rates for Ontario 2005 basket – Statistics Canada Table 326-0021.

The ASD Solution: Leaving the Municipality Behind?

In response to the budgetary challenges described above, many municipalities looked to organizational change through ASD in order to find cost savings, a practice encouraged by municipal utilities seeking to protect their revenues. Although privatization of local services is a key focus in debates on municipal supply, it is only one among several ASD options. ASD options are typically presented along a continuum from low to high independence from government (i.e. from direct delivery by the municipal department to privatization) (Good and Carin 2003; Wilkins 2005). In Ontario, these changes included a range of new business models for water supply (Bakker and Cameron 2005; Furlong and Bakker 2010).

ASD organizational reforms are commonly interpreted as being ideologically driven. At the municipal scale however, ASD emerges as a pragmatic response to budget pressures that were exacerbated by neoliberal style reforms to municipal governance. In Ontario, the key drivers for ASD, identified during interviews with utility managers, were forced municipal amalgamations, the incorporation of local hydro utilities under the *Electricity Act*, *(R.S.O. 1998, c.15)*, demands on revenue and the need for increased focus on water issues in order to keep pace with regulatory changes enacted after the Walkerton disaster. The experience in Ontario was consistent with those in other jurisdictions across Canada and abroad, where arm's length reorganization of service delivery models (or ASD) have been pursued to address particular problems (Bel and Fageda 2007; Hebdon and Jalette 2008; Warner and Hefetz 2002). This fact demonstrates that it is the strain of municipal capacity, rather than changes of ideology, that has been the most important driver for organizational changes to limit the influence of municipal governments over service delivery.

In the context of the drivers and pressures listed above, utility managers interviewed underscored what they perceived to be the most prominent limitations of the direct delivery model in meeting their concerns and thus their reasoning for pursuing ASD. First, local politics were considered to produce decisions that were not always in the best interests of water departments. Such decisions included subsidizing the property tax with the water rate, not focusing enough attention on water issues and hindering increases in water rates. Second, managers were concerned with the cost and quality of the external services that they were required to purchase from other municipal departments, chiefly human resources (HR), purchasing, and finance.

The Regulatory Solution: Provincial Regulation after Walkerton

As in a variety of other jurisdictions, water governance in Ontario has become the focus of important new regulation. New regulation and new regulatory agencies have been so widespread, that some argue that we should be talking about regulatory capitalism as opposed to neoliberalism (Levi-Faur 2005; Braithwaite 2008). With this in mind, the following section continues the case study of Ontario by exploring the effect of strong senior government regulation on municipal service delivery where municipal governance issues, such as the budgetary problems discussed above, had not been resolved.

A public inquiry was held following the contaminated drinking water disaster at Walkerton in 2000. Three major pieces of legislation ensued: the *Sustainable Water and Sewer Systems Act, (S.O. 2002, c.29)* (SWSSA), the *Safe Drinking Water Act, (S.O. 2002, c.32)* (SDWA) and the *Clean Water Act, (S.O. 2006, c.22)* (CWA). An in-depth analysis of these three pieces of legislation will not be provided. Rather, I will explore the interactions between these Acts and issues within municipal governance.

SWSSA was intended to ensure full cost recovery for municipal water and sewer systems, including the costs of source water protection and system maintenance and renewal. As part of the legislation, users were to pay the full costs and water revenues were to be ring fenced. However, the necessary regulations to support the stipulations for full cost recovery and ring-fencing were not put in place. After a six-year wait, the Ministry of the Environment (MoE) replaced the requirements under *SWSSA* with the *Financial Plans Regulation, (O. Reg. 2008, 453/07)* under the *SDWA*.

The *Financial Plans Regulation (O. Reg. 2008, 453/07)* is less demanding than *SWSSA*. It addresses only water supply and not sewage, it does not require that costs be recovered but that they are accounted for and it does not require Ministerial approval of financial plans. While acknowledging that the *Financial Plans Regulation* (2008) is a step forward, the Environmental Commissioner of Ontario expressed disappointment that it appeared to be intended to replace the more stringent and comprehensive requirements under *SWSSA* (Environmental Commissioner of Ontario 2008).

For some water managers this outcome was predictable. The partial implementation of *SWSSA* reinforced their concerns that water revenues will not be ring fenced and that they will continue to be appropriated in favor of other municipal projects. The suspicion that legislative implementation will remain incomplete lends support to the ideas that ASD is the best, if not the only, way to guarantee ring fenced revenues and adequate water prices. As one utility manager noted:

"I don't see those regs [regulations] coming for some time. It's a very hot political issue [ring-fencing] because most municipalities raid water reserves to supplement shortfalls on the mill rate [the property tax]. So that's the reason we were looking at being a stand-alone [i.e., ASD restructuring]."[6]

Several issues arose from the combination of the neglect of municipal issues within the post-Walkerton legislation (Snider 2004) and the lack of success in implementing the parts of the legislation related to ring-fencing. With respect

---

[6] Interview in Toronto (2005).

to capital investment, municipalities did increase their spending on water infrastructure in accordance with the post-Walkerton legislation (Figure 2). Yet, an examination of this investment in comparison with other key municipal financial data (Figure 1) shows that reinvestment in infrastructure is based largely on increased transfers from municipal reserve funds (Figure 1, line "Transfers from own funds") and sales of municipal assets (Figure 1, line "Other sources "). Between 1977 and 2001, "transfers from own funds" represented 46% of total capital fund revenue, compared to an average of 61% between 2001 and 2008. Over the same two periods, the average contribution from Ontario grants declined from 25% to 7.4% while the percentage of funds collected from other sources rose from 9.7% to 13.5% (Figure 1). This situation reflects a need to look to municipal reserves and assets to fund needed infrastructure, as opposed to new revenue sources or government transfers. This situation is widespread across Canada (Sancton and Young 2009).

Figure 2: Capital Expenditures for Water and Sewer for all Ontario Municipalities 1977-2008

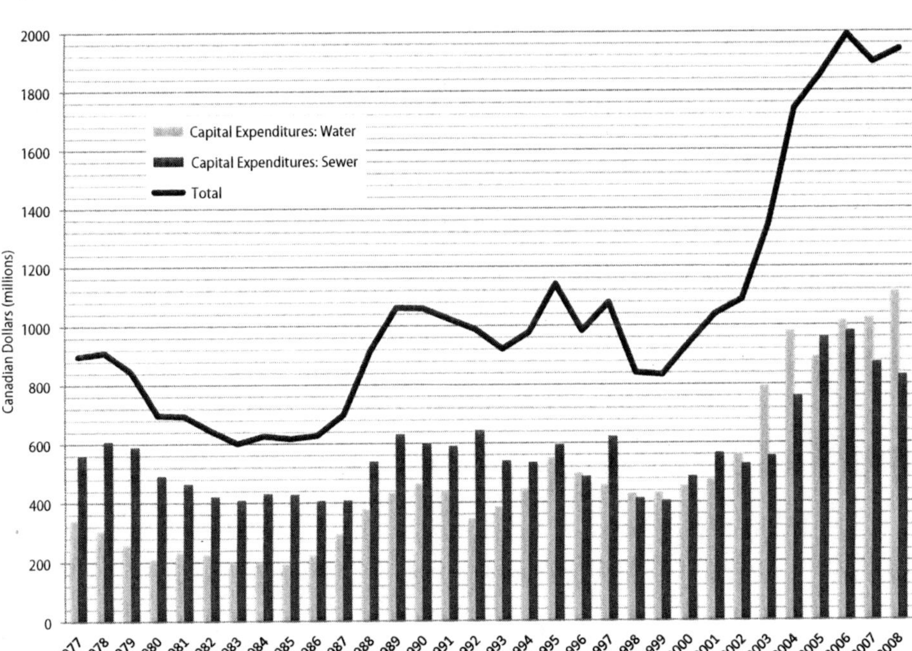

Source: Data from 1977-1999 made available upon request by the Ministry of Municipal Affairs and Housing (MMAH), Toronto, ON, data from 2000-2008 compiled from the MMAH Financial Information website (http://oraweb.mah.gov.on.ca/fir/). The data was corrected for inflation using Bank of Canada CPI rates for Ontario 2005 basket – Statistics Canada Table 326-0021.

Implementation of the post-Walkerton legislation with respect to water quality, testing, and source water protection has been successful. The downside for utilities however, is the increased financial burden of coming into compliance with this legislation. The increase in capital expenditures for water and sewer in the province are shown in Figure 2. These added cost burdens serve to make utility managers all the more conscious of the need to ring fence revenues and of ASD as a potential solution.

Interview participants in the municipalities noted the following implications of the post-Walkerton legislation. First, for water managers the legislation had increased the liability and cost burdens of supplying water. Second, the rapid pace of legislative change created the need for dedicated support services to meet the water service's increasingly specialized needs for personnel and equipment. This implies the need for specialized services from the municipal HR and purchasing departments that many managers felt required their own dedicated personnel. For both issues, ASD is seen as the solution because it would enable utilities to have budget independence as well as their own in house HR and purchasing staff.

Sufficient toSeparate? Water Supply, Municipalities and ASD

The main rational for, or goal of, the use of ASD for water supply is "de-politicization," such that utilities are able to raise sufficient revenues and to ring-fence them. Two questions are relevant to assess whether the use of ASD is appropriate to meet this goal. First, one must ask if ASD actually does in fact nullify municipal influence over water revenues. Second, even if it does do so, can ASD in and of itself ensure appropriate pricing and spending policy? In sum, in the context of municipal governance challenges, can ASD ensure the ring-fencing and full cost recovery that was not achieved through legislative solutions? Research on ASD in Ontario as well as in other jurisdictions indicates that the answer is "not necessarily." Reasons for this are discussed below.

First, strain on municipal budgets can affect water utilities even when they are self-financing. In both the US and Canada, municipalities can transfer funds from associated municipal bodies with separate revenue streams into municipal coffers through several financial instruments (Stumm 1997). In Ontario, despite stipulations for ring-fencing under *SWSSA*, water-related municipal activities are eligible for funding from water revenues. At times the relationship of such municipal activities to water may be unclear. Examples highlighted by research participants include, a program to subsidize energy for low-income residents in Hamilton (City of Hamilton 2004) and, in Toronto, the purchase of land in the greenbelt, an energy efficient downtown air conditioning program

   Reconsidering Recent Trends in Municipal Governance

and free water services for parks and recreation.[7] As one councilor put it, under municipal budget strain the temptation to construe activities as "water related" is significant:

"We get into things, you know. Where could we possibly borrow from water? Can we pull from them? If we squint our eyes up, could we call this a water project … and steal from their stabilization reserve?"[8]

Another municipal official conceded: "There's a huge temptation to take the money. Well, when you have huge budget pressures…"[9]

Poor ring-fencing is not the only problem that can persist regardless of ASD. In Kingston, despite forming a municipal corporation in 1998, the utility was unable to harmonize water rates across its new jurisdiction after the amalgamation of several municipalities (Furlong and Bakker 2011). It was not until 2007 that an agreement was finally achieved to harmonize rates across the former municipalities and the harmonization did not occur until January 1st, 2010 (Utilities Kingston 2008). This matters because rate harmonization is important for achieving social equity in funding infrastructure improvements.

While municipalities may not be able to control budgets as directly as they have previously, they can still exert a certain influence over spending and revenues. The rationale for ASD conflates service independence with de-politicization. However, "politics" can be imposed from either the municipal council *or* from utility management. Another common concern with arm's length service providers among municipal officials was that these providers tended to have higher salaries and spending than their municipal counterparts. One participant referred to them as the "cigar and whiskey club."[10] In fact, when Peterborough considered bringing its Public Utilities Commission (PUC), which provides the city's water services, back in house as a municipal department, it was unable to do so because of the higher salaries of PUC employees compared to their municipal counterparts. This speaks to a conflation of cost recovery and economic efficiency (or frugality) in the literature on ASD.

---

[7] Interview with utility management and senior corporate staff from one municipality, and a senior federal bureaucrat (2006).

[8] Interview with a municipal councilor and member of the Public Works Committee of Council (2006).

[9] Interview with a senior corporate staff person (2006).

[10] Interviews with municipal corporate staff in three municipalities (2006).

Evidence from other jurisdictions likewise indicates that organizational reform through the use of ASD cannot instill the necessary changes in municipal governance as to resolve the challenges that water managers were trying to address. This is evidenced in the widespread experience of "contracting back in" at the municipal scale due to inadequate results in terms of cost savings and efficiency (Lamothe et al. 2008; Chen 2009; Bel and Warner 2008). Moreover, it is increasingly recognized that in order to address major issues in municipal supply and to increase financial (Krause 2009) and environmental sustainability (Furlong and Bakker 2011; Kallis et al. 2010), broader changes to improve the authority and capacity of municipal governance are needed.

Conclusions

This essay highlights an opportunity to rethink approaches to municipal governance in order to solve or lessen the challenges facing water supply. The case of Ontario demonstrates that recent approaches to municipal governance that seek to improve service delivery by sidelining the influence of municipal council and staffs are limited unless long-term challenges in municipal governance and financing are addressed. Crucially, this can remain the case even when regulatory measures at the senior government level are in place.

These experiences with water supply present an opportunity to consider a more supportive and holistic approach to issues in municipal governance. As discussed in the beginning of this essay, across a variety of jurisdictions the role of municipal governments in service delivery has been questioned. Instead of addressing the challenges facing municipal governance, often policy has focused on reducing municipal government influence. By contrast, the senior government role in the regulation of a variety of issues, including water supply, has been strengthened. The water supply experience in Ontario gives pause to ask if these approaches are sufficient. The response that emerges from the above discussion underscores the importance of seizing the opportunity to improve municipal governance, irrespective of whether service delivery models are arm's length or if senior governments are fulfilling their regulatory mandates.

References

Anderson, T. L., and Leal, D. R. 1988. Going with the Flow: Expanding the Water Markets. *POLICY ANALYSIS NO. 104.* Washington, DC: Cato Institute http://www.cato.org/publications/policy-analysis/going-flow-expanding-water-markets.

Anderson, T. L., and Leal, D. R. 2001. *Free Market Environmentalism.* Revised ed. New York, NY: Palgrave Macmillan.

Association of Municipalities of Ontario (AMO). 2005. *Ontario's $3 Billion Provincial Municipal Fiscal Gap ... Needs a Solution.* Toronto, ON: Association of Municipalites of Ontario.

Association of Municipalities of Ontario (AMO), Municipal Engineers Association (MEA), and Ontario Good Roads Association (OGRA). 2001. *Financing of Municipal Water Works: Analysis and Case Studies.* Toronto, ON: Association of Municipalities of Ontario, Municipal Engineers Association, and Ontario Good Roads Association.

Bakker, K. J. 2000. Privatizing Water, Producing Scarcity: The Yorkshire Drought of 1995. *Economic Geography* 76(1): 4-27.

Bakker, K. J. 2004. *An Uncooperative Commodity: Privatizing Water in England and Wales.* Oxford: Oxford University Press.

Bakker, K. J. 2010. *Privatizing Water: Governance Failure and the World's Urban Water Crisis.* Ithaca, NY: Cornell Univeristy Press.

Bakker, K. J., and Cameron, D. 2002. *Setting a Direction in Hamilton: Good Governance in Municipal Restructuring of Water and Wastewater Services in Canada.* Toronto, ON: Munk Centre for International Studies, Program on Water Issues.

Bakker, K. J., and Cameron, D. 2005. Governance, Business Models and Restructuring Water Supply Utilities: Recent Developments in Ontario, Canada. *Water Policy* 7(5): 485-508.

Bakker, K., Kooy, M., Shofiani, N. E., and Martijn, E.-J. 2008. Governance Failure: Rethinking the Institutional Dimensions of Urban Water Supply to Poor Households. *World Development* 36(10): 1891-915.

Bel, G., and Fageda, X. 2007. Why Do Local Governments Privatise Public Services? A Survey of Empirical Studies. *Local Government Studies* 33(4): 517-34.

Bel, G., and Warner, M. 2008. Challenging Issues in Local Privatization – Introduction. *Environment and Planning C – Government and Policy* 26(1): 104-09.

Benidickson, J. 2002. *Water Supply and Sewage Infrastructure in Ontario, 1880-1990s: Legal and Institutional Aspects of Public Health and Environmental History.* [Paper commissionned by The Walkerton Inquiry] Toronto, ON: Ontario Ministry of the Attorney General.

Bird, R. M., and Tassonyi, A. T. 2001. Constraints on Provincial and Municipal Borrowing in Canada: Markets, Rules, and Norms. *Canadian Public Administration-Administration Publique Du Canada* 44(1): 84-109.

Boyd, D. 2003. *Unnatural Law: Rethinking Canadian Environmental Law and Policy.* Vancouver, BC: UBC Press.

Braithwaite, J. 2008. *Regulatory Capitalism: How It Works, Ideas for Making It Work Better.* Cheltenham, UK and Northampton, MA: Edward Elgar.

Brenner, N. 2004. *New State Spaces: Urban Governance and the Restructuring of Statehood.* Oxford, UK: Oxford University Press.

Budds, J., and McGranahan, G. 2003. Are the Debates on Water Privatization Missing the Point? Experiences from Africa, Asia and Latin America. *Environment and Urbanization* 15(2): 87-113.

Castro, J. E. 2007. Poverty and Citizenship: Sociological Perspectives on Water Services and Public-Private Participation. *Geoforum* 38(5): 756-71.

Chen, C. A. 2009. Antecedents of Contracting-Back-in a View Beyond the Economic Paradigm. *Administration & Society* 41(1): 101-26.

Chief Administration Officer. 2002. *Re: Uptake on Toronto Water Board Report.* Toronto, ON: City of Toronto.

Christensen, R. 2001. *Waterproof: Canada's Drinking Water Report Card.* Vancouver, BC and Toronto, ON: Sierra Legal Defence Fund. Available from http://www.ecojustice.ca/ reports-publications/research/.

City of Hamilton. 2004. *Water and Wastewater Budget and Business Plan.* Hamilton, ON: Available from http://www.hamilton.ca/CityDepartments/CorporateServices/ FinanceBudgetTaxes/2004Budget.htm.

de Loë, R., and Kreutzwiser, R. 2007. *Challenging the Status Quo: The Evolution of Water Governance in Canada.* In "Eau Canada: The Future of Canada's Water," ed. Bakker, K. J. Vancouver and Toronto: UBC Press. 85-103.

Downey, T. J., and Williams, R. J. 1998. Provincial Agendas, Local Responses: The "Common Sense" Restructuring of Ontario's Municipal Governments. *Canadian Public Administration* 41(2): 210-38.

Environmental Commissioner of Ontario. 2008. *Moe's Financial Plans Regulation for Municipal Drinking Water Systems.* In "Getting to K(No)W, Eco Annual Report, 2007-08." Toronto, ON: The Queen's Printer for Ontario.

Furlong, K. 2010. Neoliberal Water Management: Trends, Limitations, Reformulations. *Environment and Society: Advances in Research* 1(1): 46-75.

Furlong, K., and Bakker, K. 2010. The Contradictions of "Alternative" Service Delivery: Governance, Business Models, and Sustainability in Municipal Water Supply. *Environment and Planning C: Government and Policy* 28(2): 349-68.

Furlong, K., and Bakker, K. 2011. Governance and Sustainability at a Municipal Scale: The Challenge of Water Conservation. *Canadian Public Policy – Analyse de Politiques* 37(2): 219-37.

Fyfe T. 2004. Alternative Service Delivery–Responding to Global Pressures. *International Review of Administrative Sciences* 70: 637–44.

Gandy, M. 2002. *Concrete and Clay: Reworking Nature in New York City*. Cambridge, MA: MIT Press.

Gassner, K., Popov, A., and Pushak, N. 2009. *Does Private Sector Participation Improve Performance in Electricity and Water Distribution?* Trends and Policy Options No. 6. Washington, D.C.: World Bank.

Good, D. A., and Carin, B. 2003. *Alternative Service Delivery*. Ottawa, ON: AUCC CEPRA Project on Sector and Regional Specifics of Reformation of Budgetary Institutions.

Hansen, K. 2001. Local Councillors: Between Local "Government" and Local "Governance." *Public Administration* 79(1): 105-23.

Hassan, J. 1998. *A History of Water in Modern England and Wales*. Manchester, UK: Manchester University Press.

Hebdon, R., and Jalette, P. 2008. The Restructuring of Municipal Services: A Canada-United States Comparison. *Environment and Planning C-Government and Policy* 26(1): 144-58.

Jänicke, M. 1990. *State Failure: The Impotence of Politics in Industrial Society*. Translated by Braley, A. Cambridge, UK: Polity Press.

Jessop, B. 2002. Liberalism, Neoliberalism, and Urban Governance: A State Theoretical Perspective. *Antipode* 34(3): 452-73.

Juuti, P. S., and Katko, T. S., eds. 2005. *Water, Time and European Cities: History Matters for the Futures*. Tampere, Finland: European Commission.

Kaïka, M. 2005. *City of Flows: Modernity, Nature, and the City*. New York and London: Routledge.

Kallis, G., Ray, I., Fulton, J., and McMahon, J. E. 2010. Public Versus Private: Does It Matter for Water Conservation? Insights from California. *Environmental Management* 45(1): 177-91.

Keil, R. 2002. "Common-Sense" Neoliberalism: Progressive Conservative Urbanism in Toronto, Canada. *Antipode* 34(3): 578-601.

Kipfer, S., and Keil, R. 2002. Toronto Inc? Planning the Competitive City in the New Toronto. *Antipode* 34(2): 227-64.

Krause, M. 2009. *The Political Economy of Water and Sanitation*. New York, NY: Routledge.

Lamothe, S., Lamothe, M., and Feiock, R. C. 2008. Examining Local Government Service Delivery Arrangements over Time. *Urban Affairs* 44(1): 27-56.

Lee, T. R. 1999. *Water Management in the 21st Century: The Allocation Imperative*. Cheltenham, UK: Edward Elgar.

Lee, T. R., and Jouravlev, A. 1997. *Private Participation in the Provision of Water Services: Alternative Means for Private Participation in the Provision of Water Services*, Medio Ambiente Y Desarrollo No 2. Santiago, Chile: Economic Commission for Latin America and the Caribbean (ECLAC).

Levi-Faur, D. 2005. The Global Diffusion of Regulatory Capitalism. *The Annals of the American Academy of Political and Social Science* 598(1): 12-32.

MacLeod, G., and Goodwin, M. 1999. Space, Scale and State Strategy: Rethinking Urban and Regional Governance. *Progress in Human Geography* 23(4): 503-27.

Martin, R. L., Archer, M. A., and Brill, L. 2002. *Management and Organizational Behaviour: Why Do People and Organizations Produce the Opposite of What They Intend?* [Paper commissionned by The Walkerton Inquiry]. Toronto, ON: Ontario Ministry of the Attorney General.

McMillan, L. M. 1997. *Taxation and Expenditure Patterns in Major City Regions: An International Perspective and Lessons for Canada*. In "Urban Governance and Finance: A Question of Who Does What," eds. Hobson, P. A. R. and St-Hilaire, F. Montreal, QC: Institute for Research on Public Policy.

Montgomery, B. 2002. *The Common (Non)Sense Revolution: The Decline of Progress and Democracy in Ontario*. Creemore, ON: Mad River.

O'Connor, D. 2002. *Part One. Report of the Walkerton Inquiry: The Events of May 2000 and Related Issues*. Toronto, ON: Ontario Ministry of the Attorney General.

Osborne, D. E., and Gaebler, T. 1992. *Reinventing Government: How the Entrepreneurial Spirit is Transforming the Public Sector*. Reading, MA: Addison–Wesley.

Parker, D., and Kirkpatrick, C. 2005. Privatisation in Developing Countries: A Review of the Evidence and the Policy Lessons. *Journal of Development Studies* 41(4): 513-41.

Prudham, S. 2004. Poisoning the Well: Neoliberalism and the Contamination of Municipal Water in Walkerton, Ontario. *Geoforum* 35(3): 343-59.

Raco, M., and Flint, J. 2001. Communities, Places and Institutional Relations: Assessing the Role of Area-Based Community Representation in Local Governance. *Political Geography* 20(5): 585-612.

Raco, M., and Imrie, R. 2000. Governmentality and Rights and Responsibilities in Urban Policy. *Environment and Planning A* 32: 2187-2204.

Rhodes, R. A. W. 1997. *Understanding Governance: Policy Networks, Governance, Reflexivity and Accountability*. Buckingham, UK: Open Univeristy Press.

Sancton, A., and Young, R., eds. 2009. *Foundations of Governance*. Toronto, ON: University of Toronto Press.

Siegel, D. 1997. *Local Government in Ontario*. In "The Government and Politics of Ontario," ed. White, G. Toronto, ON: University of Toronto Press. 126-57.

Snider, L. 2004. Resisting Neo-Liberalism: The Poisoned Water Disaster in Walkerton, Ontario. *Social & Legal Studies* 13(2): 265-89.

Stumm, T. J. 1997. Comparing Alternative Service Delivery Modes: Municipal Enterprises Require Special Consideration. *Journal of Urban Affairs* 19(3): 275-89.

SuperBuild. 2002. *Organization of Municipal Water and Wastewater Systems in Ontario*. Toronto, ON: Ontario SuperBuild Corporation.

Swain, H., Lazar, F., and Pine, J. 2005. *The Case for Change in Ontario's Water and Wastewater Sector*. [Report Prepared for the Ministry of Public Infrastructure Renewal]: Publications Ontario.

Tindal, C. R., and Tindal, S. N. 2004. *Local Government in Canada*. 6th ed. Scarborough, ON: Thomson-Nelson.

Trebilcock, M. J., and Hrab, R. 2005. Electricity Restructuring in Ontario. *Energy Journal* 26(1): 123-46.

Trémolet, S., and Halpern, J. 2006. *Regulation of Water and Sanitation Services: Getting Better Service to Poor People*, Oba Working Paper Series No. 8. Washington, D.C.: Global Partnership on Output-Based Aid, World Bank.

Utilities Kingston. 2008. *Harmonization of Water and Sewer Rates*. http://www.utilities kingston.com/water/harmonization.html.

Walkom, T. 1997. *The Harris Government: Restoration or Revolution?* In "The Government and Politics of Ontario," ed. White, G., 5th ed. Toronto, ON: Univeristy of Toronto Press.

Warner, M., and Hefetz, A. 2002. The Uneven Distribution of Market Solutions for Public Goods. *Journal of Urban Affairs* 24(4): 445-59.

Water and Sanitation Program. 2011. *The Political Economy of Sanitation: How Can We Increase Investment and Improve Service for the Poor?*. Washington, D.C.: World Bank.

Wilkins, J. K. 2005. *Alternative Service Delivery.* http://www1.worldbank.org/publicsector
/civilservice/alternative.htm-2.

Winpenny, J. 1994. *Water as an Economic Resource.* London, UK: Routledge.

The Great Lakes Futures Roundtable as Watershed Governance

Rick Findlay

Director of the Water Programme, Pollution Probe, Retired

There is a widespread sense of the need to steward Canada's watersheds in ways that will secure the long-term sustainability of our water resources. There is optimism across the country that we can do this for key watersheds of concern, and there is a developing movement in that direction. There is also growing recognition of the need for rethinking the institutions and governance arrangements required to manage both the ecological and human dimensions of the watersheds on which we depend.

Some of Canada's most important watersheds, in terms of their environmental, economic, and social assets, are shared with people in jurisdictions that lie outside our national borders. The Great Lakes and Saint Lawrence River basin is one of the largest bi-national watersheds in the world. This paper describes the Great Lakes Futures Roundtable (GLFRT). The Roundtable is an informal and unofficial bi-national initiative that operates using collaborative, multi-stakeholder engagement, consensus-seeking decision- making, and watershed-based governance. If recognized by authorities and stakeholders alike, the Roundtable could improve governance in the Great Lakes basin and serve as a model for other watersheds in Canada, the United States, and elsewhere in the world. I describe the Roundtable's operating principle of open dialogue, including non-attributed discussion records, and demonstrate how this helps establish a neutral "safe-place." The use of a neutral space facilitates candid dialogue with others who may share responsibilities in the watershed or have influence on watershed leadership, decision-making or governance. Roundtable participants come from the public and private sectors. Each has influence or responsibilities in the watershed. The paper concludes that a roundtable process can play an important role in helping to develop a shared, watershed-based vision for economic, environmental, and social sustainability.

The story of the Great Lakes Futures Roundtable begins with the National Task Force on Environment and Economy created by the Canadian Council of

Resource and Environment (CCREM) Ministers (Lecuyer 1987), in September of 1987. *The National Task Force* recommended to CCREM Ministers that each province and territory form a multi-sectoral Roundtable on the Environment and Economy to bring existing organizations together to cooperate on environment-economy integration. Roundtables were subsequently established in most Canadian provinces and at the national level and came to be viewed as a timely and successful innovation. They brought together key people from various sectors with particular skills and experience, to exchange information and perspectives as they worked collectively on how to tackle challenging issues. In this case, the challenge thrown to the Canadian roundtables by the National Task Force was to wrestle with the newly emerging concept of sustainable development and to place the sustainability challenge into a contemporary policy perspective with specific suggestions on how it might become reality in Canadian jurisdictions.

Meanwhile, also in 1987, the United Nations World Commission on Environment and Development (UNCED) co-chaired by Gro Harlem Brundtland released its report *Our Common Future* (WSSD 1987). The Commission report called for the creation of new institutions that would help bring the world towards a vision of development that could be sustainable.

The so-called Canadian "roundtable process" emerged on the policy scene at about the same time that UNCED visited Canada and subsequently challenged the world to develop such new collaborative institutions for achieving sustainable development. While it should not be inferred that UNCED had the Canadian experience specifically in mind when it called for new collaborative institutions, it is likely that Canadians influenced UNCED in its work and in its call for new approaches to governance. UNCED did refer specifically to the roles played by specialized bilateral organizations such as the Canada/USA International Joint Commission.

UNCED also influenced the thinking and awareness of Canadians. In Canada and around the world environmental policy development has been based on an emerging appreciation for the benefits of following a multi-stakeholder, collaborative, consensus-seeking approach to policy development. The roundtable process was found to be a timely means to assist the development and implementation of practical policy solutions to challenging issues including the emerging concept of sustainable development. Benefits of the roundtable process came to be appreciated by many, including the author who served as Director of the Ontario Roundtable on Environment and Economy. The Ontario Roundtable served as an effective mechanism for developing consensus among individuals who came from different backgrounds and who brought complementary perspectives, information, experience and energy to shared challenges then being faced by six sectors of the Ontario Economy (Agriculture, Transportation,

Urban Development, Energy and Minerals, Forestry, Manufacturing, and Native Peoples).

The Ontario Roundtable on Environment and Economy (ORTEE) was created in 1988 by Premier David Peterson. In 1990 the Roundtable released its Challenge Paper (ORTEE 1990). The paper laid out a vision with a set of six guiding principles and suggested a specific approach to achieving sustainable development for Ontario. With its Challenge Paper and through the establishment of Sector Task Forces (which themselves were also consensus-based, multi-stakeholder roundtables), ORTEE challenged the six key sectors of the Ontario economy to respond with specific suggestions on how to achieve sustainability for their sector.[1]

Focusing on the Great Lakes and Saint Lawrence River Watershed

In 2002, the author, then Director of the Water Programme at Pollution Probe, undertook the challenge to better understand and address the sustainability needs of the Great Lakes watershed. A good place to begin was to undertake a fresh examination of global experience in managing freshwater as well as either marine or freshwater coastal areas that were shared by different countries or jurisdictions around the world. Pollution Probe, working in partnership with the United Nations International Network for Water, Environment and Health (UNU-INWEH) and supported by several partners, held a week-long international conference in June, 2002 in Hamilton, Ontario called Managing Shared Waters. The conference was attended by 440 delegates from 38 countries. It provided international and Great Lakes participants with a contemporary assessment of the capacity needs of those working towards the sustainable development of marine and freshwater coastal zones, particularly in trans-boundary situations. The initiative also provided stakeholders working in shared freshwater and coastal areas with tools and approaches that they could use to address the issues arising in their communities. A case study on the Great Lakes basin (Heathcote 2002) prepared for the Managing Shared Waters conference concluded:

"In summary, progress toward Great Lakes water management goals is limited in part by weak capacity to measure and understand the physical, chemical and biological systems

---

[1] The Sector Task Force responses then were used by the ORTEE to produce its overarching "Restructuring for Sustainability" final report, in 1992. The sector-based, multi-stakeholder challenge process proved to be a very engaging and effective technique for bringing groups of experts together to collectively respond to what was increasingly being recognized as an important economic, environmental and social priority.

*of the vast and complex Great Lakes. This limited capacity in turn can limit the capacity
– and perhaps the will – to develop effective legislation tailored to particular problems.
This situation is particularly critical because of the Basin's rapidly ageing infrastructure
and its ballooning population. As population grows and more land is converted from
agriculture to urban development, pressures on infrastructure can only escalate. It is
clear that significant government restructuring and budget cuts in the mid-1990s have
contributed to these problems; it is equally clear that those cuts have prompted a fundamental re-thinking of the entire challenge of environmental management. New technologies and new partnerships offered the promise of solutions over the longer term but in
the immediate future, there is a need to coordinate research and monitoring activities
across borders and levels of government, as a basis for the development and enforcement
of better legal systems, and the implementation of effective infrastructure. Although the
International Joint Commission's boards and agencies, and the Remedial Action Plan
program, provide some opportunities for this coordination, results have been mixed, and
more effective coordination mechanisms are urgently needed."*

The Hamilton Statement which emerged by plenary session consensus on the
last day of the Conference challenged *inter alia* the North American Great Lakes
community "to continue to innovate on institutional arrangements and other
mechanisms, such as Round Tables, and provide leadership in capacity building
and sharing best practices" (Pollution Probe 2002).

Adding an important bi-national perspective, the International Joint Commission (IJC) Science Advisory Board, in its 2001-2003 Priorities Report, found
"there are no institutional mechanisms for policy development or consensus
that are effective on a bi-national basis to address policy opportunities for the
Great Lakes" (IJC 2003). The report recommended that the Parties should "further develop bi-national institutional mechanisms to enhance bilateral cooperation and coordination for air, land and water management in order to implement
a truly ecosystem approach for water quality management that involves local,
state/provincial and federal governments" (IJC 2003).

At the same time, the Great Lakes and Saint Lawrence River institutional landscape was growing and evolving to meet a wide array of perceived needs. Most
of these institutions emanate from government bodies such as Environment
Canada and the U.S. Environmental Protection Agency, as well as numerous
other Federal and State/Provincial agencies and departments and bi-lateral
agencies such as the International Joint Commission (IJC) and the Great Lakes
Fisheries Commission (GLFC), which were established by treaties between the
United States and Canada. Other institutions include the State of the Lakes Ecosystem Conference (SOLEC), the International Association for Great Lakes Research (IAGLR), political organizations such as The Council of Great Lakes Governors (CGLG), non-governmental organizations including Great Lakes United

       The Great Lakes Futures Roundtable as Watershed Governance

(GLU) and the Council of Great Lakes Industries (CGLI). In addition, there is also the Great Lakes Commission (GLC), a public agency established under the Great Lakes Basin Compact. The Great Lakes Basin Compact is an interstate agreement to promote the orderly, integrated and comprehensive development, use and conservation of the water resources in the Basin and The Great Lakes-St. Lawrence River Water Resources Regional Body which was established by the Great Lakes Governors of Illinois, Indiana, Michigan, Minnesota, New York, Ohio, Pennsylvania and Wisconsin, and the Premiers of Ontario and Quebec (Compact Council 2005).

It seemed to the author that the respective agendas of this range of Great Lakes institutions were increasingly focused on the individual missions of the various organizations and institutions rather than on a common agenda in accordance with a shared vision. Few of these key organizations and institutions shared a common or coordinated mandate or vision, other than being Great Lakes focused in some way.

In early November 2002, these observations were confirmed through discussions between the author and employees of several of these institutions. When asked, all agreed that some new kind of neutral, watershed-based forum of key individuals would be helpful for establishing and achieving a fresh vision for the sustainability of the Great Lakes watershed as a whole.

Thus, the idea of a Great Lakes Roundtable emerged as a neutral forum where participants would be able to meet, exchange information and discuss issues, ideas and opportunities. The Roundtable was envisioned as a "safe" place where no attribution of remarks would be recorded in the meeting record which would subsequently be developed and shared for accuracy. This characteristic of the Roundtable was developed to allow participants to have honest discussion. This "safe place" idea emerged from the author's perception that in many bilateral or multilateral Great Lakes meetings participants often found themselves having to defend, advocate and position for opportunity or advantage in support of positions being taken by their employer agency or institution. As a result, participants had little or no opportunity to stand back and collectively think about constructive ways to advance the sustainability of the watershed as a whole. Simply put, there was a perceived need for a neutral place where talented, dedicated individuals could meet and talk openly, without attribution and without feeling the need to advocate or defend the positions of their employer, organization or agency. In order to highlight the importance of the unique "safe place" function provided by the Roundtable it was determined that the GLFRT would not be a voting body, a debating society, an operational body, another self-serving "stakeholder" nor a threat to any institution. Rather, it should be an arm's length initiative owned by nobody but shared by everybody.

The first meeting of what became known as the Great Lakes Futures Roundtable was convened on April 3, 2003. At the first meeting, organizers said they hoped the Roundtable would be an informal gathering of individuals who, in their personal and professional capacity are committed to achieving a common vision for the bi-national Great Lakes basin through discussion and action. The same approach was taken to guide subsequent meetings of the Roundtable. To date (March, 2012), the GLFRT has met 17 times; the most recent meeting was held in Windsor, Ontario March 16-17, 2011 and was co-chaired by the author.

The first meeting of the Roundtable focused on the need for:

- a more effective bi-national coordination mechanism among Great Lakes institutions;

- a common and agreed upon collective vision, recognizing that each organization has a different role and purpose but largely complementary interests;

- a fresh, energized, forward-looking, more inclusive Great Lakes initiative that would bring direction, attention and new resources (public and private) to the basin;

- increased public and private investment in the region;

- an international (global) perspective on the Great Lakes; and

- a more integrated (Great Lakes) water management system.

At this meeting, concern was also expressed that unilateral Great Lakes initiatives were emerging in jurisdictions and institutions around the basin, suggesting a gradual move away from commitment to the notion of common bi-national enterprise and the absence of a shared vision. Two examples of such initiatives include the Regional Collaboration of National Significance initiative and the U.S. Great Lakes Interagency Task Force that were signed into law in 2004 by U.S. Presidential Executive Order. While these actions represented significant investment in protecting the Great Lakes by the United States, a comparative or analogous investment initiative has not been undertaken by Canada.

The absence of a shared vision and of a communal "safe place," to facilitate discussion regarding the sustainability of the Great Lakes watershed, was seen to be inhibiting the development of a shared agenda for watershed sustainability.

Attendees at the first Roundtable meeting confirmed that they would participate as individuals but individuals who also happened to work with organizations including the International Joint Commission, the Great Lakes Commission, the Great Lakes Fisheries Commission, the Great Lakes Water Quality Board,

Environment Canada, Council of Great Lakes Industries, University of Toronto, and Pollution Probe. Some were retired "elder statesmen," but all were personally concerned about the future sustainability of the Great Lakes watershed. The participants discussed the need to review the Great Lakes Water Quality Agreement and for public participation during such a review. The Great Lakes Region was determined as the geographic scope for the Great Lakes Futures Roundtable. The Great lakes Region was defined as the eight States and two Provinces within which the integral Great Lakes and Saint Lawrence River watershed is located. All Roundtable participants attended the meeting at their own discretion and their own cost. Rick Findlay, Gail Krantzberg, and Mike Donahue were nominated to oversee completion and distribution of the first meeting notes and to lead the group towards possible next steps.

Meanwhile, in May, 2003, the General Accountability Office (GAO) in the United States released a Report on the Great Lakes that seemed to echo the sentiments of the Roundtable organizers. The report found that the Great Lakes lacked a unified vision, an overarching strategy, and proper funding (GAO 2003).

Organizers believed that the roundtable process helped fill gaps that existed quite naturally between the numerous Great Lakes institutions and official public and private sector agencies, companies and organizations. Such gaps occurred especially when representatives of those organizations at the outset felt the only option they had was to do the best job they could to advance the official positions of their employers. The Roundtable provided an opportunity to develop a shared vision and to advance an overarching strategy for the long term sustainability of the watershed. It did this by exploring productive and synergistic solutions to shared challenges, finding mutual "win-win" solutions for achieving the sustainability needs of the watershed and exploring ways that the participants in the roundtable process can work together to implement these solutions. The Roundtable continues to exist and meets as participants wish. As of October 2012 it had met 17 times.

The Roundtable and Watershed Governance

Governance in the Great Lakes and Saint Lawrence River watershed has been a particular subject of discussion by the GLFRT. The need for more effective coordination, management and accountability mechanisms among Great Lakes Saint Lawrence institutions and organizations has been discussed at virtually each meeting. In order to understand who was responsible for what and accountable to whom, in 2005 the GLFRT created a one-page Great Lakes mosaic or framework that graphically described the connections and relationships between the key Great Lakes Saint Lawrence River institutions. This framework continued to evolve and improve and a revised version was produced June 1, 2007 (Appendix 1).

The GLFRT recognized the need for a fresh, collective, bi-national vision that would bring new direction, attention, and resources to public and private sector organizations, institutions, and companies in the basin. In October 2007, the GLFRT released its *Great Lakes Saint Lawrence Vision, Mission and Goals* (GLFRT 2007). This two page document offers a sustainable development vision that includes environmental, economic, and social goals. It recognizes the importance of new strategies to preserve both the natural and economic capital needed to help turn the Great Lakes Saint Lawrence River region from a "rust-belt" into a "blue belt."

Based on the Roundtable's approach and vision, in late 2006 and early 2007 Gord Miller, the Environmental Commissioner for Ontario (ECO), and the author collaborated to hold a series of invited roundtable meetings as well as evening public forums on the future of the Great Lakes. The events were held in Kingston, Windsor, Hamilton, Thunder Bay, and Toronto. One of the goals of the initiative was to present and discuss the GLFRT Vision and to gather reaction. A backgrounder report on the series of Ontario meetings was released and the office of the Environmental Commissioner also prepared other supporting documentation (ECO 2006).

With the advice and assistance of the Great Lakes Futures Roundtable, the International Joint Commission convened a stakeholders' roundtable in 2009 where it was noted that the GLFRT Vision would likely transcend the current tradition of the Great Lakes Water Quality Agreement. As put forth in the Roundtable's Vision the IJC 2009 stakeholders' roundtable concluded that achieving water quality in the Great Lakes would require taking a broader approach that would include social, economic, and other complementary measures. Support was given at the stakeholders roundtable for a high-level "summit" event or "leaders' roundtable" that could be held in support of this broader approach, seeding an idea that would come to fruition in 2011.

Based on the encouragement and support of the Roundtable members at the 2009 meeting, a Steering Committee of the Roundtable met in 2010 at Ann Arbor to advance work towards such a high level "Summit" or "Leaders' Roundtable" event. Dubbed the "Great Lakes-Saint Lawrence River Regeneration Conference" the purpose of the meeting was to engage with leaders from various sectors in the region and allow them to bring a shared level of understanding, acceptance and receptivity to the kinds of socioeconomic, cultural and environmental changes that will be necessary to attain sustainability in the Great Lakes region.

The Roundtable Steering Committee proposed that the 2011 leaders' summit should take a 100 year timeframe for its vision and focus on how to attract the new capital and investment needed to make the region the most livable, healthy and sustainable place in the world in which to invest.

Also in 2010, the author learned of a separate proposed Great Lakes summit event that was in the planning stages led by Dr. Matthew Mendelsohn from the Mowat Centre for Policy Innovation at the University of Toronto in conjunction with John Austin of the Metropolitan Policy Program at the Brookings Institution. It was suggested the efforts of the two summit initiatives be merged. That was subsequently accomplished by cross-connecting advisory committee memberships.

In September 2010, the Brookings Institution published *The Next Economy: Economic Recovery and Transformation in the Great Lakes Region* (Vey et al. 2010). From June 21-22, 2011, with advice and input from the Roundtable the Brookings Institution and the Mowat Centre for Policy Innovation co-chaired a Great Lakes Saint Lawrence Region Summit that took place in Windsor/Detroit. About 250 delegates from across the region participated in the policy discussions and the discussion was captured in *The Vital Commons: a policy agenda for the great lakes century* (Hjartarson et al. 2011)

It is not possible to measure the direct influence of the Great Lakes Futures Roundtable or the Great Lakes Saint Lawrence Region Summit. Credit for the outcomes that resulted from the summit fall to those Roundtable participants who took the risk for the event and had direct responsibility for it. While the author would conclude that the outcomes of the Summit reflected success from a roundtable point of view, it was never a priority of the Roundtable to measure its own success or to seek credit for progressive actions that were subsequently taken by others connected in any way to the Roundtable. Some might conclude this reflects a weakness in the roundtable model while others might suggest this is exactly the kind of helpful role an arms-length mechanism should play in seeking to ensure the sustainable development of a watershed.

Benefits, Challenges and Water Opportunities Associated with a Roundtable Approach:

Benefits

This discussion of benefits, challenges, and opportunities is derived from observation by the author and discussion with Roundtable members and as such should not be construed as a rigorous analysis. However, it is fair to say that the

Roundtable did bring "traditional environmentalists" together with business leaders and economists to learn about the economic strengths of the Great Lakes Saint Lawrence River watershed region. The Roundtable learned from one of its members, who was familiar with an analysis done by World Business Chicago, that the region represented the third largest economy in the world, after the United States and China (WBC 2011). This kind of information was recognized as important in order to better understand the sustainability of development in the Region. The Roundtable expanded its education on the economic and social aspects of the region by reaching out to new participants who could bring additional information and depth in these areas. For example, in November 2006 the Federal Reserve Bank in Chicago hosted one of the Roundtable's meetings. Representatives of the bank brought interesting and relevant economic and social information to participants for their consideration. It is fair to credit the Roundtable collaborative process with stimulating a number of positive new studies and initiatives. The Roundtable brought new perspectives and ideas regarding future possibilities to audiences in the region that might not have come together if the Roundtable had not provided a forum to discuss the long-term sustainable development of the region.

The multi-stakeholder, consensus-based, collaborative roundtable model is an example of a "bottom-up" mechanism that complements the more traditional "top-down" kinds of institutions and initiatives that are often expected of governments and private-sector based organizations. The roundtable process has also fostered discussion and development of an emerging potential initiative on the international Great Lakes scene. At its recent meetings, the Roundtable held discussions around a "challenge" process that could conceivably emerge in response to a 100-year vision initiative created by Chicago architect Philip Enquist and his team at Skidmore, Owings, and Merrill (SOM 2011a). This discussion is not complete to date. However it can be followed on-line at "The Great Lakes Century: Toward a Vision" blog (SOM 2011b).

Challenges

Financially sustaining the operations of the GLFRT has been a challenge. Roundtable leaders have had to seek financial support due to the fact that the Roundtable does not show up on the organization chart of any participating (or non-participating) institution. On the other hand, the Roundtable's success has largely been due to the fact that the GLFRT does not compete with public and private institutions.

Gaining institutional acceptance and comfort with new collaborative, multi-stakeholder, consensus-based mechanisms such as roundtables will be key to enabling these mechanisms to fulfill their potential in terms of contributing a new approach to water management in watersheds everywhere. Roundtables should not be a threat to any of their potential participants. Rather, they should be considered a mechanism for all to listen and be heard and to seek a workable consensus about how to protect and sustain shared watersheds.

Water Opportunities

Watershed boundaries rarely align neatly with political boundaries as a watershed can spread over a number of jurisdictional boundaries at municipal, provincial/state, and national levels. Long-term watershed management and protection will require the engagement and involvement of a range of individuals and organizations, both public and private, in order to find solutions for watershed protection that will be truly sustainable and that reflect the long-term environmental, economic and social needs of people, businesses, institutions, and communities.

Protecting the future long-term sustainability of watersheds will require new approaches and new kinds of both formal and informal management mechanisms that will help sustain watersheds through a collaborative approach. Such an approach will need to involve "governments" at all levels along with other key public and private organizations that share an interest in the sustainability of a watershed.

Conclusions

A collaborative, multi-stakeholder, consensus-seeking, watershed-based roundtable process would likely be beneficial in addressing the governance challenge of watershed management especially in a multi-jurisdictional context. Appropriate public, private, and non-governmental interests need to be engaged and involved in finding practical solutions to sustaining the watershed as well as the public and private interests that must thrive sustainably within the watershed.

A roundtable process should be a complement and not a threat to responsible governments or other institutions. A roundtable process can facilitate the emergence and development of a more distributed and, at the same time, a more integrated approach to watershed management that includes "top-down" as well as "bottom-up" dimensions.

A shared, long-term (100-year) vision for watershed sustainability will be helpful in raising the energy, enthusiasm and widespread recognition of the importance and benefits of protecting and sustaining watersheds. Such a vision should be based on a broadly shared ethic of stewardship and responsibility for sustainable watershed management.

Appendix 1

The Great Lakes / St. Lawrence
Environmental Governance Framework 2007

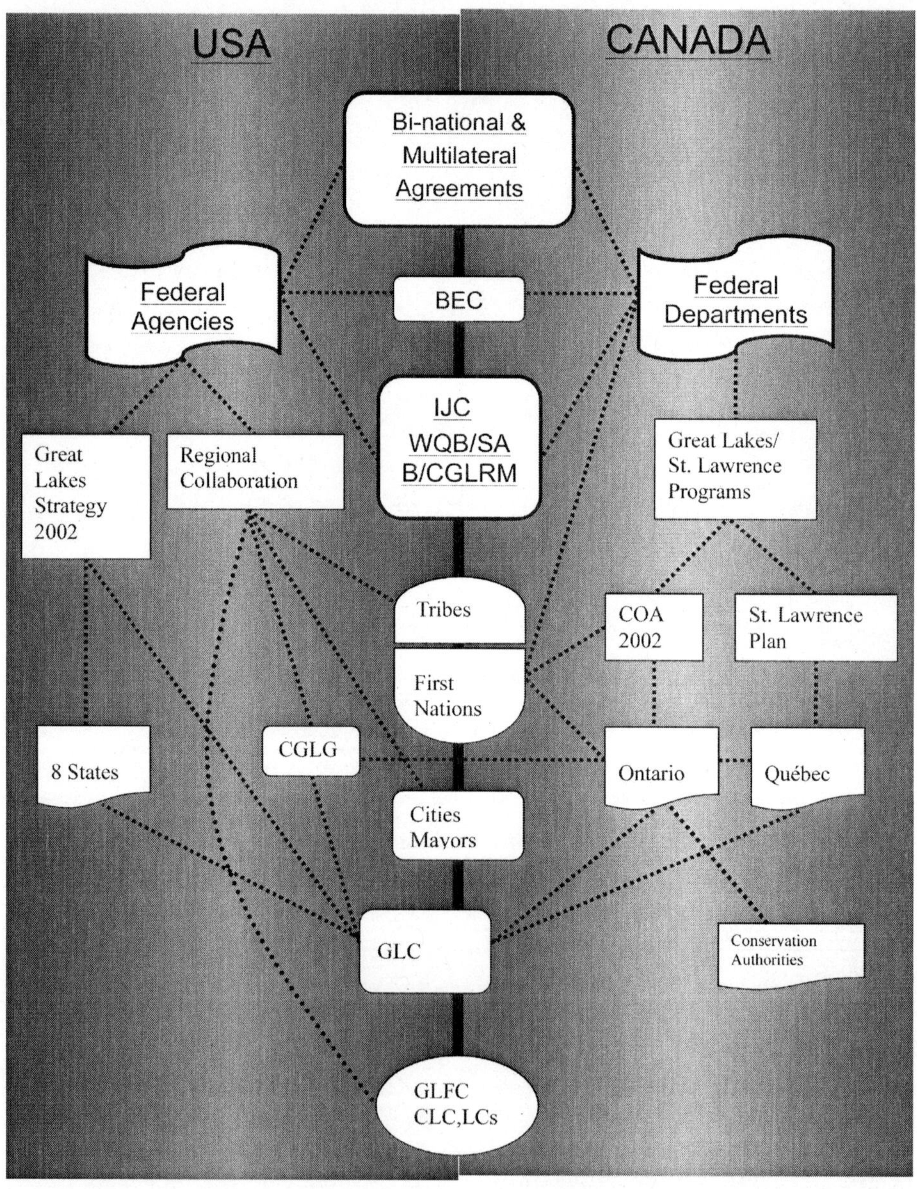

References

Environmental Commissioner of Ontario. 2006. *Great Lakes Roundtables: Backgrouder.* Toronto, ON: Environmental Commissioner of Ontario.

Great Lakes Futures Roundtables. 2007. *Great Lakes Saint Lawrence Vision, Mission and Goals.* Available from http://www.pollutionprobe.org/old_files/Reports/greatlakes vision.pdf.

Great Lakes-St. Lawrence River Basin Water Resources Council. 2005. *Great Lakes – St. Lawrence River Basin Water Resources Compact.* Available from http://www. glslcompactcouncil.org/Agreements.aspx#Implementing%20Agreements.

Heathcote, I. W. 2002. *Capacity Development in the Laurentian Great Lakes Basin Ecosystem.* Paper presented at Coastal Zone Canada 2002: Managing Shared Waters – Towards Sustainable Transboundary Coastal Ecosystems, Hamilton, ON, June 23-28.

Hjartarson, J., Mendelsohn, M., McGuire, N., and Shloberg, R. 2011. *The Vital Common: A Policy Agenda for the Great Lakes Century.* Toronto, ON: Mowat Centre for Policy Innovation.

International Joint Commission (IJC). 2003. *Priorities 2001-2003: Priorities and Progress under the Great Lakes Water Quality Agreement.* Ottawa, ON: International Joint Commission. Available from http://www.ijc.org/en_/news?news_id=226.

Lecuyer, G. 1987. *Report of the National Task Force on Environment and Economy.* [Report prepared for the Canadian Council of Resource and Environment Ministers], Ottawa, ON.

Ontario Round Table on Environment and the Economy. 1990. *Challenge Paper.* Toronto, ON: Queen's Printer for Ontario.

Pollution Probe. 2002. *Hamilton Statement on Managing Shared Waters.* Paper presented at the Coastal Zone Canada 2002: Managing Shared Waters – Towards Sustainable Transboundary Coastal Ecosystems, Hamilton, ON, June 23-28.

Skidmore, Owings, and Merrill, LLP. 2011a. *Recognizing a Global Resource: The Need for a 100 Year Vision for the Great Lakes and St. Lawrence River Region. Chicago.* Chicago, IL: Available from http://thegreatlakescenturyblog.som.com/recognizing-a-global-resource.

Skidmore, Owings, and Merrill LLP. 2011b. *The Great Lakes Century – toward a Vision.* Skidmore,Owings & Merrill, LLP, http://thegreatlakescenturyblog.som.com.

United States Government Accountability Office (GAO). 2003. *Great Lakes: An Overall Strategy and Indicators for Measuring Progress Are Needed to Better Achieve Restoration Goals.* [Report GAO-03-515 prepared for Congressional Requesters] Washington, D.C.

Vey, J. S., Austin, J. C., and Bradley, J. 2010. *The Next Economy: Economic Recovery and Transformation in the Great Lakes Region*. Metropolitan Policy Program at Brookings. Available from http://www.brookings.edu/research/papers/2010/09/27-great-lakes.

World Business Chigago. 2011. *Great Lakes St. Lawrence Economic Region Profile*. World Business Chigago, http://www.worldbusinesschicago.com/news/great-lakes-st-lawrence-economic-region-profile.

World Commission on Environment and Development. 1987. *Our Common Future*. New York, NY: Oxford University Press.

Water as an Opportunity for Social Engagement
The Tale of Two Strategies

Hilary Van Welter

CEO Ascentia, Director, ReWild!

"Empty your mind, be formless, shapeless – like water. Now you put water into a cup, it becomes the cup, you put water into a bottle, it becomes the bottle, you put it in a teapot, it becomes the teapot. Be water, my friend."

This quote of Bruce Lee, martial artist and actor, offers us the idea that water itself is transformational and holds a key to opportunities for new thinking, new concepts, and learning. The notion of "being water" symbolizes a different relationship with water and nature, one that brings respect for the intelligence embedded in water. What if we all began to take on some of water's characteristics to help move towards a better future? What if we were to unfreeze like water in Spring and become more open to reshaping our behaviour and embrace new possibilities?

If we are able to become like water, we have the potential to access a new framework and context that can provide us with a refreshing lens through which view to areas that are socially vulnerable, for example our suburbs. Taking on the characteristics of water could provide us with an innovative methodology with which to arrive at new solutions to the difficult issues that pervade our suburban lives such as disconnection, disengagement, increasing unemployment, and high dropout rates. For example, water could provide the thinking to help us transform suburban life as we know it and create communities that even our rebellious teens would want to live and work in. We could take down our suburban fences to create flowing, connected spaces from our backyards; replace the pavement in school yards and crescents with sparkling pools of neighbourhood art, food, and flora gardens, or even create a network of "innovation estuaries" that blends the arts, science, and technology to deliver practical solutions to redesigning suburban life at home and around the world.

This is the type of thinking that emerged through two social innovation projects that I have designed and conducted over the past six years which combined social innovation and water. These projects were aimed at tackling behavioural change and mindset shifts through belief transformation. The first project, entitled The Naked Truth, was an initiative that took place in the Ontario Lake Simcoe Watershed in 2006. The project sowed the seeds of a provincial protection act and the allocation of major federal funding for Lake Simcoe. As described in detail below, The Naked Truth continues to guide progressive change today. The second was a forward-thinking initiative of the Regional Municipality of York who, rather than conduct the usual public consultations, opened its doors and invited the public to help shape its 40 Year Water Strategy known as The Long Term Water Conservation Strategy.

In both these cases, water was not just an object or a topic, but a player in the design and delivery of social innovation. The term social innovation differs significantly from the very popular approach of social marketing used by many environmental organizations. Social marketing uses a "push" philosophy. Key information is custom delivered to various target groups to promote specific behaviours. The behaviours promoted are meant to achieve a specific social good. Social innovation on the other hand uses a "pull" approach. Images of radically new mindsets and new approaches are sent out to the public as an invitation to join the social change, or social innovation. The majority of innovations are conducted by individuals who do not fit into the easily identified segments of a population. Rather than being part of a targeted audience or demographic, they lie in the cracks between the sectors. These individuals are often at the fringe of their disciplines and/or society and inspired by radical change and new possibilities. The "pull" approach draws in the ideas and people from different sectors and disciplines described above in order to create change. By targeting the large, easily identified segments of the population, the marketing approach tries to alter groups of people whose behaviours are difficult to change. In doing so the marketing approaches ignore those people who are less easily defined and who are arguably more in favour of the new mindsets and behaviours that are needed to produce social change.

Changing people's behaviours around water is truly a challenge because water plays a large part in our lives yet many people do not think about their water use. The Naked Truth and York Region's Long Term Water Conservation Strategy identified the need to understand the drivers behind these behaviours. The field of Epigenetics, the study of changes in gene activity that are not caused by changes in the DNA sequence, is opening up new frontiers in understanding human behaviour. Bruce Lipton, a cellular biologist, has undertaken extensive research on how our cells function. His findings are documented in such publications as *The Biology of Belief* (Lipton 2005) and *The Wisdom of Your Cells* (Lipton 2006). Healers throughout the ages have worked with the premise that people's belief programming, inherited through generations, acts as a complex default program, primarily in our subconscious mind, that controls our behaviour. Science is now catching up.

To achieve true behavioural change we must uncover and restructure hidden beliefs. In order to understand these hidden beliefs and how they affect behaviour, we use what is called design thinking. Design thinking defines a problem in a way that reframes the issue. It uses keen observation followed by developing and testing hypotheses before deciding on a solution.

Water, both mysterious and practical, inspired me to delve into the realm of social innovation, belief transformation, and design thinking. Water has continuously proven to inspire social movements. The following two initiatives provide examples of this.

The Naked Truth

Like many stories of significant change, this tale began with a simple act: the dipping of a paddle into the water of the Maskinonge River that feeds into Lake Simcoe, approximately 75 km north of Toronto, Ontario. It was the summer of 2004. Among the people in the canoes that morning were, Jane Meredith and Annabel Slaight. Each time they put their paddles into the water they came up with large amounts of weeds. The journey quickly became more of a workout than either woman had bargained for. In a moment of desperation, Jane declared that the condition of the river, which reflects the condition of the lake, was totally unacceptable. Something had to change.

Lake Simcoe (Figure 1) was formed by glacial melt-water and the remnants of a much larger, prehistoric lake known as Lake Algonquin. One hundred years ago Lake Simcoe housed the largest ice industry in North America because of the lake's pure spring fed waters. Today it is loaded with phosphorus, choked with weeds, and full of invasive species. Jane and Annabel's first move was to form a non-profit organization called Ladies of the Lake.

The organization's first project was a celebration of the beauty of Lake Simcoe. The decision to highlight and honour the beauty of the Lake was both heart-felt and strategic. It was believed that people were growing tired of the typical environmental messaging of gloom and guilt. The women decided to reconnect people to the Lake by showcasing its beauty. In this spirit the women's first project took the form of a "cheeky not cheesy" calendar of naked women whose bodies blended with the landscape to showcase a year in the life of the Lake Simcoe

Figure 1: The Lake Simcoe Watershed

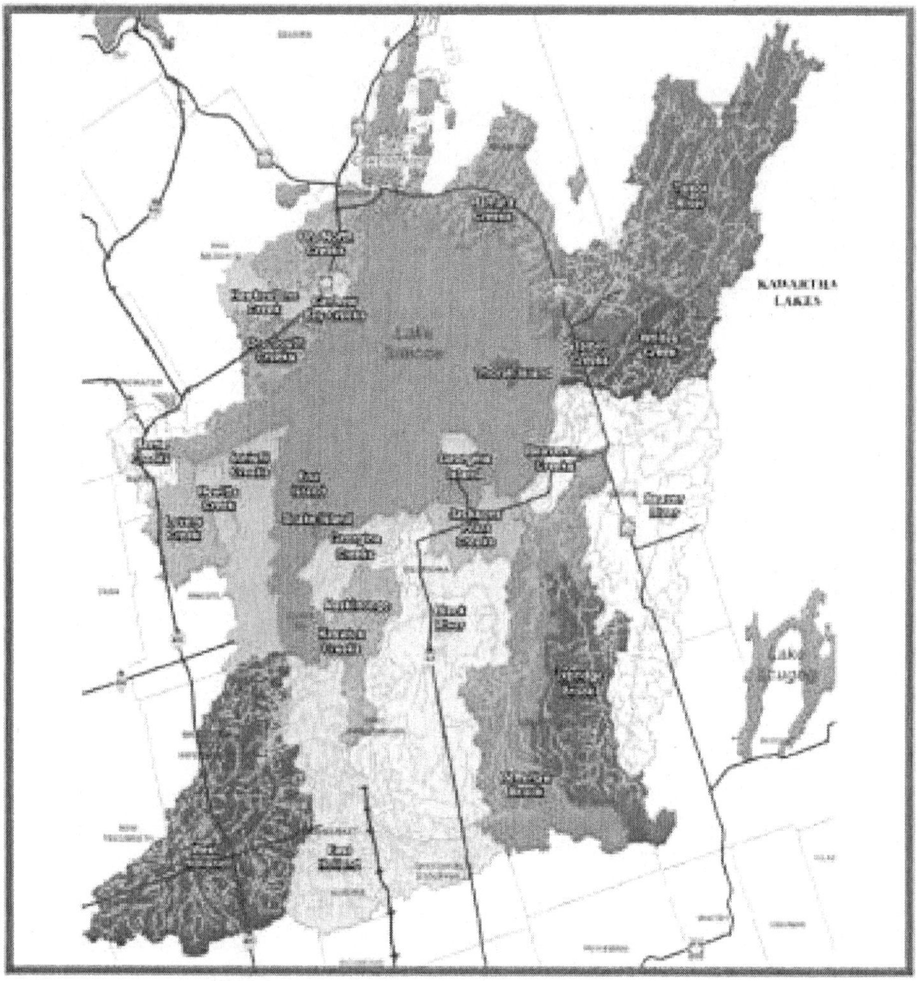

Source: Lake Simcoe Region Conservation Authority. 2014. http://www.lsrca.on.ca/maps/.

watershed. The calendar was a highly professional, tasteful, whimsical, and compelling way to view the natural exquisiteness of the Lake Simcoe watershed.

The 2006 Ladies of the Lake Calendar was highly successful, raising over $250,000 through sales and donations. It had also created a real buzz around the watershed. To capitalize on this attention, Jane and Annabel formed a partnership initiative between Ladies of the Lake and Windfall Ecology Centre, entitled The Naked Truth.

The Naked Truth had three distinct components. The first was a research project that brought together the often conflicting and diverse scientific research that had been conducted on the watershed. Several reports existed that contained differing assessments of the phosphorus loading condition. There was a need to interpret these scientific findings and to present the findings in a way that the general public could understand. To fulfill these needs, the partnership generated a report entitled *Going Behind the Science of Lake Simcoe* (Chabot et al. 2006). It was published with the goal of turning awareness into action. This report brought awareness to the collection of issues facing the Lake and watershed. It provided sets of actions that could be undertaken by several of the key stakeholders of the Lake including the citizens, governments at all levels, developers, and businesses.

To understand the findings it is important in order to have a sense of the characteristics of the Lake Simcoe watershed. The watershed comprises 23 sub-watersheds and 22 municipalities. In 2001 it was home to over 350,000 residents and was estimated to have a population of over 500,000 by 2021. The watershed includes about 3,303 square kilometres sweeping north from the Oak Ridges Moraine through parts of York and the Durham Region, the City of Kawartha Lakes, and Simcoe County. Twelve-thousand cottages, 24 Conservation areas, 3 provincial parks, and just under 2 000 farms are located along its shoreline. The watershed is very active, containing urban, rural and suburban dynamics. The findings of the Report confirmed that increased infrastructure including housing and roads as well as increased boat usage had resulted in phosphorous loading, invasive species, and overall natural degradation. What was perhaps most startling was the interconnectedness of the causes and impacts that formed a web of destruction. Table 1 outlines the indicators of change that were impacting the lake, along with the possible causes. It was clear that a single solution would not work. The lake was in need of a holistic solution that utilized the "ecosystem thinking" approach.

The second component of the Naked Truth was called The Naked Truth Summer of Events. These events were guided by four organizing principles: (a) apply an ecosystem mindset, building on the natural intelligence of Mother Earth; (b) utilize fresh vision and fresh governance to harness the power of community; (c) communicate inventively as the watershed is very complex; and (d) revitalize relationships and reconnect with and renew nature's cycles. The partnership designed four sessions aimed at sharing the research results in a way that would mobilize people to create positive change. While the indicators and causes of change could seem overwhelming, this component of the project was based on the idea that action by citizens had the potential to change the tide.

Table 1: Indicators of Change and Possible Causes from the Naked Truth Report

Indicators of Change	Phosphorus	Global Warming	Invasive Species	Urbanization	Storm Water Runoff	Altering Natural Cover	Boating	Loss of Natural Areas	Fluctuating Water Levels
1. There are more and more houses.				X					
2. The natural shorelines have been replaced.				X	X	X		X	
3. Sometimes my well runs dry.				X	X	X		X	X
4. There are signs posted saying I cannot swim today.	X			X	X	X		X	
5. They say there is less phosphorus, but there are still lots of weeds.	X	X	X	X	X	X		X	
6. There are more weeds and algae, and the lakebed is covered in goo.	X	X	X	X	X	X		X	
7. There are new species in the lake and the water is clearer.	X	X	X	X		X	X		X
8. I am catching lots of Lake Trout, what's the problem?		X	X	X	X	X	X		X
9. There seems to be fewer turtles and frogs.		X	X	X	X	X		X	X
10. The weather patterns are changing.		X							

Source: Chabot et al. (2006).

During two weekends in July of 2006, citizens came out to four unique expeditions around the Watershed to experience both the degradation and the beauty of the lake and its surroundings. Citizens paddled in canoes *on* the water, travelled in antique cars *beside* the water, went aboard cranes and helicopters *above* the water and went diving *under* the water. The research results were shared through a set of Naked Truth Cards that were especially designed for more manageable and tactile interaction. The participants heard from experts of all types including academic scientists, developers, police divers, and farmers.

The expeditions captured the good, the bad, and the ugly through the participants' lenses. The physical experience with the lake and watershed solidified the need for change within each participant. In this way the expeditions helped the partnership recruit a commitment from individuals, businesses, and governments to take part in an action plan to restore the lake. The participants suggested actions that then were sorted and clustered into Priority Areas. In August of 2006, 100 citizens went aboard The Serendipity Princess steamship to sail the waters of Lake Simcoe and to finalize what was to become *The Naked Truth Citizens' Action Plan to Save Lake Simcoe* (Van Welter and Slaight 2006).

This Action Plan, published in October 2006, contains a vision for lake living that is seemingly simple, yet entails a deeper meaning. The vision slogan was drink it, swim it, fish it, love it. Drink it means to purify our water, our minds, our public policy, and our forms of growth. Swim it means to provide access to the Lake as well as its rivers and shore for enjoyment. Fish it means honouring the natural habitats and natural economic activities. Love it means to be guided by nature, to save our souls and to save the lake for the sake of our children.

The Action Plan contains eight Priorities with over 130 proposed solutions that can be mixed and matched across the Priorities to create innovative projects. The Priorities are: better policy/legislation, sustainable development, the next generation, community eco-nomics, treasuring the lake, science and research, lake unity, and healthy shorelines. One of the bold possibilities of this plan included combining a water science centre concept with a water museum and a water park. The museum would teach and celebrate the cultural aspects of water in all forms while the science centre and water park would provide hands on experiences as well as experiments and scientific knowledge.

This was the first time that a comprehensive strategic plan had been created for a watershed by citizens. Many plans had been developed by various levels of governments, NGOs, and the Lake Simcoe Region Conservation Authority, but none had brought all the major issues, along with potential solutions, under one plan. Also, the ideas had come from people who had experienced a truly emotional connection to the vision and were committed to implementing the actions. For example, the water science centre and water museum, and park idea has evolved into the Ontario Water Centre (http://www.ontariowatercentre.ca/). Many plans sit on shelves because of a lack of emotional connection. This plan came from feeling, touching, and connecting with the water rather than from a mere intellectual exercise.

The Citizens' Action Plan was published in a unique fan deck format to allow people from across the sectors to "play" with the ideas in order to create projects, programs, and initiatives that would mobilize change. This fan deck was distributed throughout the watershed to municipalities, NGOs, The Lake Simcoe Region Conservation Authority, provincial and federal departments, and interested businesses. It served as an initiator as well as a reminder of the types of actions citizens would support and get involved with. The initiative was a success! On December 8, 2008, the *Lake Simcoe Protection Act* was passed. The significant role that the citizens had played in this effort was recognized on the floor of the legislature. This Act was followed by a Lake Simcoe Protection Plan that has citizen involvement at its core. Many of the ideas from the fan deck were integrated into the Protection Plan and the ensuing Strategy.

The federal government also realized the benefits of supporting the Lake Simcoe "movement" and announced a $14 million Lake Simcoe Clean Up Fund in 2007 that was to be topped up to $30 million. These funds were allocated to projects that helped protect, restore, and create critical aquatic habitats as well as habitat for associated species populations and to projects that reduced the lake's phosphorous content. Funding was also allocated to providing improved environmental information for decision making through research and monitoring.

While the money was well received, what made this initiative groundbreaking was again the involvement of citizens in the decisions of where and how the money would be spent. The Naked Truth initiative and the collective efforts of citizens and NGOs to get an Act passed set a precedent for the level of citizen involvement that would be necessary for all future initiatives. This precedent laid the groundwork for the establishment of the PROPEL (Protect and Preserve the Environment of Lake Simcoe) Committee. The PROPEL Committee was made up of representatives from NGOs and citizen groups from around the Lake Simcoe watershed who reviewed all the funding submissions once they had been screened by the Science Committee. This Citizen Committee was the final recommending body to the Minister of the Environment as to which projects should be funded and to what extent. Allowing the grassroots determine where the greatest priorities were and allocating the funds accordingly was a rather radical idea.

The Lake Simcoe Protection Act and Plan, as well as the Lake Simcoe Clean Up Fund, are not the end of the story but rather the beginning. The Naked Truth spawned other social innovations such as a youth initiative entitled WASTE Films that involved a Lake Simcoe Youth Film School, Film Festival and the Where Waters Meet Conference. This innovative project lead by teens, enabled by professional filmmakers, and mentored by Lake Simcoe, used film to help shift the way we live (www.wastefilms.ca). The youth developed a deep relationship with the lake when they realized that, like them, the lake was undervalued and had no voice; like them, the lake was in need of healing and; like them, the lake had unique and amazing attributes to offer the local community. This mentorship by the lake has proven to be a unique component of subsequent youth initiatives that have had amazing results. One such result has been the social innovation project called ReWilding which was born out of discussions at the Where Waters Meet Conference. ReWilding recently completed its first pilot and is currently turning urban and suburban stewardship on its head through a new methodology and set of techniques. These are profiled in a new iBook entitled ReWilding Keswick Creeks.

The Naked Truth was an inspiration for change. It served to showcase that people care about where they live and are willing to get behind positive action. The Naked Truth was *for* something, not against. This was the distinct difference from the typical environmental perspective of guilt and redemption. The plan

Water as an Opportunity for Social Engagement

profiled exciting new possibilities across the sectors and encouraged collaborative action, a rather novel approach in 2006. The Naked Truth sowed the seeds for a new relationship between people and nature, one of partnership. Being a partner with nature requires that we use different intelligences and senses to truly connect to the elements that have been around far longer than we have. Nature has amazing insights if we are ready to listen. We must listen deeply.

York Region's Long Term Water Conservation Strategy

In many respects the social innovation that helped create York Region's Long Term Water Conservation Strategy is the next evolution of the Naked Truth and what it spawned. Tracey Carrigan, the Manager of Environmental Education & Promotion for the York Region's Environmental Services Department, had become intrigued by the WASTE Films project after attending both the WASTE Film's Gala, an event to showcase the films, and the Where Waters Meet Conference as an invited guest. Tracey saw the potential of this type of unique community engagement and became a valuable partner in the ReWilding Keswick Creeks pilot project.

At the same time, Tracey was preparing to embark on the significant process of developing a 40 year water strategy for York Region. York Region is centrally located in the Greater Toronto Area (GTA), directly north of the City of Toronto, Ontario, Canada. York Region covers 1,756 square kilometres (678 square miles) and is comprised of nine local municipalities. It is the only Region in the GTA without direct access to Lake Ontario. This strategy began out of a need to expand the sewage flow capacity and intra-basin transfer of drinking water while maintaining the Region's commitment to sustainable development and long-term water conservation. The Long Term Water Conservation Strategy (LTWCS) required consultation with lower-tier municipalities, the Southeast Collector Advisory Committee, the public, relevant government agencies, and the Central Regional Office of the Ministry of Environment (MOE).

Having been part of many initiatives involving public consultation and education, Tracey identified the consultations as an opportunity to go about stakeholder engagement in a fundamentally new way. To support the Region's work, I conducted an initial study with the community to determine topics that may be controversial during stakeholder engagement. This research identified that:

- There was "Plan Fatigue." There had been a wide range of plans developed at the Regional and Municipal levels, all of which included "public consultation." Because of this, there was a possibility that engagement would be met with a "not another plan" response.

- The public had been overloaded with "Environmental" and "Sustainability" messaging and was becoming desensitized to it.

- The current context for water was outdated yet engrained.

- Current awareness and education campaigns to shift peoples' relationship with water, and therefore their behaviour, were not working.

- There was a large gap between desired behaviours and engrained beliefs.

York Region wished to engage its stakeholders in an authentic process that would help shape water use throughout its nine diverse municipalities over the next 40 years. When scanning the environment to determine the current relationship people have with water, we found that water is viewed as a commodity, a resource to be saved, and the subject of Canadian myth that we have an abundant, unlimited water resource, which often means we take water for granted. This relationship and its ensuing mindset had guided the development of water related strategies for the past number of decades, but presented significant challenges in looking forward 40 years. As Albert Einstein is often quoted as saying, "We can't solve problems by using the same kind of thinking we used when we created them." To change the thinking we had to change the mindset. To do this we turned to social innovation.

Social Innovation

Social innovation is a blend of unique collaborations and creative actions, between different sectors, that are all aimed at changing the way people think and see. To understand the dynamics of social innovation we undertook a review of its best practices. We chose to focus on the different experiences and insights of a few of the pioneers of social innovation as outlined in the *Open Book of Social Innovation*. The book shares ways to design, develop, and grow social innovation.

One of the most significant findings of our review was the focus on *establishing a new public*. Rather than trying to "convert the masses," social innovation sends up flares that speak to a new way of thinking and seeing everyday things. For example, by sending out messaging that shows a new way to think about water and our behaviour towards it, those who are attracted to the messaging begin to spread those perspectives. This approach also allows people to grow the perspectives in creative new ways across all sectors therefore reaching a broader audience. This new public is not a passive consumer but an active player. They help to create the social innovation by taking the messages and incorporating them in their own way. By taking this approach the Regional Municipality of York was able to tackle the deeper issues of mindset shift and valuing of water while identifying a path forward that allows for the protection, preservation, and use of water.

 Water as an Opportunity for Social Engagement

The following objectives were created to guide the design and implementation of the stakeholder engagement for the 40 year Long Term Water Conservation Strategy.

- Change the Canadian narrative with respect to Water.

- Involve citizens in uncovering the new narrative and generating innovative ideas.

- Transform the social context through street level innovations and engagement.

- Develop a powerful brand that tells a new story for water.

- Develop a framework for a multi-year process of social innovation.

The objectives were designed to address the role of water in a changing economy and society. This was a tall order for a stakeholder engagement that was to be completed in five months. Diversity of two way streams were needed through which we could draw people to us for meaningful conversations, as well as sharing new insights and ideas as part of unfreezing our relationship with water. Our goal was to draw people in for meaningful conversations that would unfreeze the current relationship with water, while at the same time generate new insights and ideas shift the context and narrative around this key resource that everyone is so familiar with, but know little about. The stakeholder engagement included a Best in Class Review, a Special Report on Water, a Youth Film Project and public events, a website, public "Water Cafes," and "Water Future" sessions.

One of the most important goals at each event was to help people create a new relationship with water. To help the stakeholders envision a different future, with respect to water, we attempted to connect them with water through topics that mattered to them in their daily lives. We asked questions such as: how are we going to live and work in the future, what does a "Blue Region" look like, and how do we reinvest in our suburban communities to build a sustainable future? These questions ignited a dynamic dialogue. While exploring the question what is water's role in helping you achieve these visions of the future, people dove into their imaginations, drew out rich ideas and consequently positioned water as a vehicle of change. This vision is outlined in the Water Futures section below.

Impressions of Change

Much can be said about these various engagement activities. However, perhaps the best way to share their power is in the lasting images of the people who came out and shared their deep concerns and love of water in their own unique way.

Having designed and facilitated these sessions, I would like to share certain observations that I feel reflect the true nature of this engagement. In each and every case, the people who were drawn to these sessions were thirsty for new and inspired conversations about their future (social innovation). The events provided fresh lenses through which to tackle tired issues such as development and planning (design thinking). Most important of all, water gained a respect, reverence, and admiration that may not have existed before. This laid the groundwork for an implementation plan that positioned water strategically as a driver for change instead of just as something ordinary that comes out of our pipes, taps, and toilets.

As an opening to the Water Café on Celebrating Water, we were fortunate to have members of the Chippawas of Georgina Island First Nation perform a blessing and smudging ceremony to open the doors to fruitful conversations. It was quite a sight to see people from a wide range of cultural groups experience this sacred ritual for the first time. It was a hopeful beginning to the very fertile discussions that were had throughout the Water Cafes and Water Future Sessions.

In the Rehearsal Hall at Markham Theatre, our Superbia Water Café explored redesigning suburbia. Here we witnessed a citizen take on a member of the development industry. His message was that it was critical for that industry to truly listen to the consumer whose needs were changing. Water innovation, conservation, and efficiency are needed as basics in new development not as expensive options. This created quite a loud exchange but, it unleashed some great ideas. We also had a twelve year old ask for a translation of what one of the academic adults was saying. The simplification ended up sowing the seeds for the inspiration goal of the LTWCS.

It was a dark and very stormy fall night for our Blue Region Water Café, which resulted in a small yet intimate conversation. The café took place in the majestic foyer of the McMichael Art Gallery in Kleinberg. The questions and discussions that emerged around the future of education, health, and business were highly significant. Such discussions included one about the baggage and possible limitations that the word "conservation" carries and another regarding the fact we need to be green in order to "go blue."

In the original home of the Eaton Family, Eaton Hall, the planners met with the citizens to explore how a new context for water could renew other planning initiatives. It was refreshing to see the way water could add a new dimension and integrate distinctly different plans.

We had wonderful input from children. The theme of storms ran through a number of art works. There was an inherent enjoyment and awe of the rain, lightening, and the unpredictability of weather. The young artists celebrated the many forms of water while showcasing it as a unique combination of light and colour. The power and humour of water also showed up in the form of an artistic water view of the 2010 DreamWorks Animation film "How to Train Your Dragon." When asked if you were a water drop, what would you wish for, we had a wonderful range of wishes. One that stood out the most was, I would marry Thunder. These expressions reflected a connection to water that was magical rather than merely functional. It showed how water can bring out our resilience as well as imagination. What a gift that was.

Water Future Sessions

Having collected all of this input, we now had to analyze, cluster, and organize it into a workable format for the Long Term Water Strategy. The result was an overarching vision with a series of goals, guiding principles, success criteria, and actions. Using the method of putting actions in "time buckets" (0 to 5 years, 5 to 10 years, 10 to 20 years, and 20 years and beyond) and then sifting, sorting, and strategizing, the implementation strategy for the LTWCS was set.

Broadly speaking, the first five years were about piloting and testing. Years 5 to 10 were implementation and years 10 to 20 focused on continuous improvement. The 20 years and beyond held a template of where the participants wished they would be. From there the strategy for the next 20 years would be launched. The main points included:

- A new economic structure with indicators that reflect healthy people, planet and economy;

- Decisions and standards based on integrated trends in demographics, climate, employment and economic development;

- Clear indicators of a cultural shift that are anchored in an appreciation for the full value of water and our fresh water assets;

- A global water institute that leads the way for the next 20 years; and

- Green and blue construction is common with engrained green business standards and practices.

These indicators of what a 20 year future could look like will act as signposts in the development of Regional policy over the coming years. What makes the above noteworthy is that water is embedded as a player in the economic structure; water is a vehicle that brings together and connects 4 diverse areas: demographics, climate, employment and economic development; water is a key player in a very necessary cultural shift in what and how we value; water is the focus of learning for York Region and around the world; and water helps shift the standards of business. In these scenarios water is not an issue left on its own in terms of quality, quantity, and use, but instead it is entrenched in all fundamental issues.

The Long Term Water Conservation Strategy was created by bringing the key components from stakeholder engagement together with an extensive technical and best practices component that was created during the strategy development.

In reflecting on the process to develop the LTWCS, what stands out the most is what happened when York Region threw open its doors for people to come and share their thoughts, feelings, expertise, knowledge, wishes, and dreams about the future of their water. This was not merely a series of engagement sessions to gauge public reaction to a strategy. The stakeholders were key players in helping to shape the strategy itself. There was a trust that the "new public," formed through this engagement, knew what would ignite their various communities as well as get people excited about a new context and relationship with water. There was also a trust that having the stakeholders lead the way would be a key factor in the sustainability of the strategy over the years.

Another key dynamic of this engagement was the use of design thinking and social innovation to help people re-imagine a new future. The stakeholders did not regurgitate another version of the current reality but instead made use of cutting edge technologies, cultural innovations, and new learning techniques to re-imagine a new future for York Region through water.

"Water has always been a connector, drawing people and communities together. As a source of life water flows throughout all significant issues; it is a messenger of climate change, a co-creator of energy and, in York Region, it is an agent of innovation and change" (The Regional Municipality of York 2011).

As part of this innovation and change, the LTWCS has an ambitious target of "no new water" for the Region. This means that usage in 2051 across all sectors should be equivalent to usage in 2011 despite growing demand and an estimated increase of 800,000 people. Significant conservation and innovation will be needed to realize this scenario. The stakeholders however have already created a pathway of how to make that happen, guided by the vision provided in *Water: Reviving The Way We Live*.

The Confluence of the Two Tales

While these examples are quite different, the two tales share a great deal in common. Most importantly, both stories depict how water links people together and provides us with opportunities to connect people with social, economic, and environmental topics that need attention.

                    Water as an Opportunity for Social Engagement

We are gradually becoming aware that we must question some of the fundamental aspects of our society. In these times of change we need new choices because existing solutions are becoming obsolete. Design thinking gives us an exciting new way of tackling problems. Rather than defaulting to our conversion approach in which we make the best choice from our available options, design thinking can help us to explore new alternatives, new solutions, and new approaches that haven't existed before. Design thinking also allows us to integrate opposing ideas such as exploring people's spiritual relationship to water while at the same time seeing how water can help make sound financial decisions. Add water to design thinking and social innovation and the opportunities are taken to a whole new level. But why do we need to do this?

The majority of our mindsets come from an industrial era, with assembly-line, mechanical, cookie cutter thinking. The majority of our current institutions that guide our lives are based on these crumbling mindsets, or models. Water, like people, is merely a utility in these old frameworks. We desperately need to dismantle these old institutions and replace them with organizational forms that reflect 21st century thinking, thinking that is inspired by a combination of the new sciences and the ancient knowledge of the natural world. This is a massive undertaking, but water could lead the way. Here is an example.

After presenting the two case studies profiled in this chapter at a course I teach entitled REpower Ontario, I asked the following question: What role can water play as an agent of change? While all the answers were valuable, one response truly stuck out: water could help dismantle the prison system. After waiting a couple of minutes to let that idea sink in, the class explored what that statement could mean. We ended up identifying ways that the properties and characteristics of water could inspire practical water projects as well as changes to the prison culture based on water's transformational powers. These ideas involved shifting the dynamic inside prisons to be places of true rehabilitation rather than punishment; for the inmates to engage in entrepreneurial, sustainability and environmental science research activities. Finding a sense of meaning, along with new skills would enable inmates to contribute to society rather than be a drain on it. Interestingly these ideas are now coming alive in San Quentin, California, and in various institutions in Washington State.

This is what is meant by true water thinking. There are enormous opportunities to deal with significant social issues by calling into existence a new public who wish to tackle the root causes and not just the symptoms. However, this takes daring and courage. One has to be like Indiana Jones and put your foot out over the open chasm, trusting that you won't tumble into the abyss. In both these tales, water and fresh energy rose up to meet our feet and we were able to move to our next stop on the journey.

Water and People have a unique partnership that holds enormous potential to shape a brilliant future for Canada. To start, be water my friend.

References

Chabot, J., French, R., Kopperson, B., Rodgers, G., Slaight, A., Welter, H. V., and Verma, R. 2006. *The Naked Truth - Going Behind the Science of Lake Simcoe.* ed Welter, H. V. Sutton West, ON: Windfall Ecology Centre.

Lipton, B. H. 2005. *The Biology of Belief: Unleashing the Power of Consciousness, Matter and Miracles.* Santa Rosa, CA: Mountain of Love/Elite Books.

Lipton, B. H. 2006. *The Wisdom of Your Cells: How Your Beliefs Control Your Biology.* Boulder, CO: True Sounds.

The Regional Municipality of York. 2011. *Long Term Water Conservation Strategy.* Newmarket, ON: The Regional Municipality of York.

Van Welter, H. and Slaight, A., eds. 2006. *The Naked Truth Citizens' Action Plan to Save Lake Simcoe.* Sutton West, ON: Ladies of the Lake and Windfall Ecology Centre. Available from www.windfallcentre.ca or www.lakeladies.ca.

Waterlution

Seanna Davidson, Ph.D.

Research Fellow, Systemic Governance Research Program, Monash University, Australia

On occasion, the bright ideas generated in conversation, that build with energy and passion, are able to create a place for themselves, and influence the systems they see are in need of change. Waterlution set out to change the way we were talking about water; to move from siloed sector-based, technical conversations, to cross-sector, inter-generational, inspired and creative facilitated dialogue that achieves more than another report. Having recently celebrated its 10-year anniversary, Waterlution has accomplished much.

To date, 59 workshops have been held in almost all provinces and territories; 3500 young leaders have participated; 50+ Associates have been trained in facilitation; local Hub networks have emerged for community building on water in major cities and the 2nd Water Innovation Lab took place in September 2013. Waterlution is a Canadian national not-for-profit organization whose purpose is to inspire pattern-making and pattern-breaking change towards a healthy and sustainable relationship with water. It achieves this purpose through delivering curated journeys that help young leaders find their water voice, and to share what they know across sectors and viewpoints. Waterlution has grown from kitchen table conversations to an organization that has engaged people from across sectors, perspectives and generations with a belief that deep systemic change happens as individuals build understanding across viewpoints and cultures, share knowledge, and develop broader perspectives through open, cross-silo dialogue and community building.

In this chapter, we explore the story of Waterlution, the core ingredients that formed its foundation, how it evolved in response to the lessons along the way, and the impact it has had on individual water leaders. The focus and purpose of Waterlution as an organization is both an example of a social water innovation in and of itself, but the story also shares important lessons on how a water organization can be emergent, innovative and responsive to the complex dynamics of water decision-making.

What is Waterlution and Where Did It Come From?

In the early 2000s Karen Kun and Tatiana Glad were seeing momentum build around water issues, both in Canada, and globally. The World Summit on Sustainable Development (WSSD) would make water a focus of discussion, while 2003 was named the international year of water. Kun and Glad had met in Montreal during University as active AIESECers (the largest student organization in the world) and both were studying for their commerce degrees. They had a shared passion for the natural environment, and saw how business could be a positive driver toward environmental sustainability, and both attended the WSSD. Coinciding with the WSSD experience, each were involved in a global community of facilitators called "Pioneers of Change" that experimented with process, as well as an "art of hosting" community of practitioners. Together Glad and Kun were looking for an opportunity to contribute their skills to the water sphere and saw two specific needs relating to water. The first related to what they felt was a major challenge to effective water policy and management. The problem was based in our decision-making strategies; the way we currently make decisions and communicate is grounded in a system that is out-dated and no longer effective. Yet it is what is culturally understood, and therefore, for the most part goes unchallenged. The uni-directional teaching, memorizing and reciting found in our education system, how our government system is styled by statement making, rather than conversation, even how people gather – conferences are platforms for presenters, not dialogue. Kun and Glad felt that in order to solve complex issues, the more we have to bring our knowledge into the discussions and then have genuine conversation. To do that requires the use of our emotional selves combined with our intellectual selves (emotions being, empathy, kindness, laughter, tears perhaps at times, discomfort, elation). All of these emotions, combined with knowledge and experience on the topic at hand, allow for people to connect and for trust to be built, before it is possible to embark on solving complex issues.

The second related to who engaged in the decision-making process and how it was facilitated. Often when facilitators were called into a water process, while they had the skills to facilitate problem solving, they lacked the thematic content expertise. Kun and Glad observed how better outcomes, collaboration and innovation happened when those with extensive water knowledge were engaged with facilitated design. Kun found that if facilitators lacked the content expertise, it was very hard to get the respect of participants. Ultimately, this would affect their capacity to steer participants towards creative and effective solutions. This premise would become the foundation for Waterlution, the combination of content *and* process. Kun and Glad felt that only with the presence of both content and process could meaningful dialogue and problem solving on complex water issues occur. They set out to create an organization that would do just that.

Setting the Frame and Creating the Space

Kun and Glad were intentional about the design and capacity of the organization, wanting it to be both nimble, and have great capacity for growth. As Kun noted, "because there isn't anywhere on the planet where you can't talk about water or that you can't have an interest in having good water resources." They drew on a number of different ideas to create a framework for Waterlution. They found inspiration in the chaordic principle outlined by Dee Hock, the founder of VISA, and author of *Birth of the Chaordic Age* (Hock 1999). Hock defines chaordic as a system of organization that engages both chaos and order. This thinking permitted space to create some intention about the goals of the organization, while allowing the process to emerge through experimentation and learning. The story here highlights how Waterlution continued throughout its development to stretch and grow, and experiment.

Knowing they wanted to equally include content and process, they sought to build skills and expertise in both. While they had already been working with facilitation and the art of hosting practices, they wanted to continue to expand and refine their capacity. Kun shares what this looked like in the early days, "we were always testing out, we were hosting things in our living rooms, we were basically continually trying to hone our craft by practicing different skills and engaging with different people and building our network." So before even offering "Waterlution" events they were prototyping different processes. Alongside they recognized that they had to build their credibility around water issues. While both had been engaged in environmental issues, they lacked a specific focus on water and the Canadian context. Kun who would become the Executive Director, would spend the better part of the next few years travelling across the country, meeting with experts, learning at conferences and building a network with practitioners living deeply with water challenges across a host of sectors. Kun comments about the importance of "showing up," "in the beginning, [it] was about me being able to show up in all parts of the country and develop networks. Being able to say, 'yeah, I'm going to be in the North West Territories,' it's amazing how you can meet 20 people, where you would have been able to speak to one or two if you just said, 'can I phone you?'" These connections would also bring in different perspectives on what was needed and helped to shape the organizations' approach. An example of the importance of these conversations is highlighted in how the "Future of Water" workshop model was developed. In 2003 Corporate Knights magazine approached Waterlution to collaborate on a water-focused issue. Kun and Glad connected with Bob Sandford (EPCOR Chair of the Canadian Partnership Initiative for the United Nations' Water for Life Decade) to lead their advisory board for the issue, and this began a long-standing relationship between Waterlution and Dr. Sandford. The very first full

Waterlution workshop came from Sandford and Kun's first face-to-face meeting in Invermere, BC, and was recorded, like all important insights, on a napkin. With Sandford sharing the important issues around Glaciers and the Bow Valley and Kun sharing her network of young leaders and facilitation skills, the Future of Water workshop model was born. Taking each of the important elements of their first meeting, their napkin model evolved to a 3 day retreat style workshop with young leaders and water professionals from across sectors, and a facilitation team to support the dialogue and learning, while focused on a particular theme and hosted in locations across Canada.

From the beginning Kun and Glad wanted Waterlution to be about a multi-stakeholder space, where participants would connect outside of their silos, and make deep connections with people holding different perspectives, all within the shared context of both the scientific and human aspects of water. One participant shared, "I like that Waterlution purposefully brings together leaders from all stages and walks of life to explore issues from different perspectives. It provides a much needed space where we can keep watering our ideas and nurturing our connections." As part of this, one of Waterlution's core values is of cross-sector dialogue, where respectful conversation can take place around large-scale topics (from oilsands to fracking to agriculture), and where all perspectives are given voice. Another participant commented, "I think Waterlution does an admirable job of bringing stakeholders to the table who are usually at odds, and having a healthy, pragmatic, and respectful conversation about the real issues. I haven't really seen this done very well in any other context." Kun sees this as an important component of building opportunities – the approach can't be focused on opposing something, but instead, it must be open – to new ideas, perspectives, but also the realities of our current context. It's what Kun calls, "creating the amazing." As she sees it, "we have the ability, the resources, the skills, the education, to create amazing, and we believe that culturally people are willing and able to follow amazing." By being open and engaging across perspectives, we have greater potential to creating the amazing – together. Part of creating a constructive space for the dialogue is also about being attuned to the balance between the perspectives. At each event, Waterlution strives to have a balance between those working across different sectors. Kun shares that the challenges of this kind of dialogue, is to keep interesting, bold ideas flowing, and not to facilitate participants to compromise to end up with the lowest common denominator. This is where the skills of hosting and facilitating are paramount. The focus of the organization however, is not to be a negotiator, it is to generate ideas for water.

Identifying how this cross-sectoral dialogue would happen was also part of the process. An important influence was the fact that people bond more if they've shared an experience, and so a retreat type of experience started to emerge as an opportunity for the Future of Water workshops. Kun notes "very few people in life, will not enjoy a fire, some tomfoolery, and a nice environment to eat and sleep." Waterlution workshops are somewhat like camp, they are held in spaces that are rustic, but comfortable, are situated in the natural environment, while still being close enough to "water contexts" where there is still opportunity for resources guests join and field trips for the experiential learning component. Being intentional about not only the content and process, but also the physical and social space that their events happen in has come to be another important element of Waterlution's programs. It can facilitate deeper relationships because participants interact on an inter-personal level, instead of on a more formalized professional level. One Waterlution participant commented, "Waterlution provides a unique discussion environment, where participants break down organizational and disciplinary silos to build new bridges based around particular issues and solutions. The mix of field visits and innovative facilitation creates an engaging learning and connecting experiences. At events, students and young professionals dialogue with resource guests as peers- when experts are typically placed on podiums – this way enabling knowledge to flow in all directions."

Waterlution associates design everything from when people arrive into the "experience" until they exit. Yet designing the experience does not mean there are expected and specific outcomes, rather that the skills of the associates are used to allow the process to unfold organically and to work with the group through the uncomfortable parts. Kun shares, "we actually love that part [the uncomfortable part] the most, yet it is what most people, organizations, conference, gatherings try to avoid. That is where the magic, opportunity, authenticity and innovation lie. When groups feel on the edge of discomfort yet 'supported enough' by the hosting team. And wow oh wow…when you get through the hard conversations, and remain together, then after that, and only after that (this is usually into day 2 or 3) that the best ideas, innovations, collaborations develop. Most people start nodding their heads a lot, smiling a lot on the last day – most people understand now the journey they have just experienced."

Another core principle of Waterlution is play. In their book, *Play, Playfulness, Creativity and Innovation*, Bateson and Martin (2013) identify play as "behaviour that is spontaneous and rewarding to the individual; is intrinsically motivated and its performance serves as a goal in itself." Kun comments "when we play together we remember the love of water that has brought us together." Through play, it is possible to build the excitement and energy people have about a resource that they care about, while building strong relationships and creating a space where creativity can thrive – it's what helps get us to the "amazing." In their research Bateson and Martin found an important link between play, creativity and solution building. "Play is also about breaking away from established patterns and combining actions or thoughts in new ways. Play is an effective mechanism, therefore for encouraging creativity and hence facilitating innovation." Waterlution brings in elements of purposeful play, to build community, but also to encourage creativity and innovation in their community of water leaders who are working towards a shared goal. This process is captured by Nassbaum, in his book *Creative Intelligence: harnessing the power to create, connect and inspire*, when he says "silly play on its own doesn't lead to innovation. The best ideas emerge out of a process that involved a variety of players who trusted one another working together toward a specific goal" (Nassbaum 2013).

Evolution of Work

The popularity of the workshops continued, and a number of valuable insights were drawn relating to process. One in particular spoke to the network that Waterlution was beginning to build across the country. While it was often the names of the resource guests that drew participants in, feedback would focus on their experience, rather than one element. Participants would comment on the sense of community, support and playful environment that inspired them. "I always leave the workshops energized and feeling more connected to a national network of change makers. Through the network I have made friends and discovered opportunities that have influenced the course of my career." Over time, there came greater calls for opportunities to keep these connections and inspired momentum going. Another insight was that the young people attending yearned for more interactions with those more experienced than them, but in an environment where personal relationships could actually be built, as opposed to just a trading of cards. Kun recognized that the way you are introduced to people is often a deciding factor for the kind of relationship that can be generated. In small-scale informal settings, conversations can take more of a mentoring tone and participants can come away feeling they've made a connection they can follow up on for guidance and support. All of which helps generate a stronger community of water professionals. A Waterlution participant shared, "Waterlution has allowed me to build a network of passionate individuals working on water issues in Canada."

While the workshops grew, so too did the Waterlution team. Alongside the growth of the workshops was interest in participating as a facilitator, those who had experienced weekend workshops wanted to learn more and have deeper engagement in the Waterlution process. This suggested there was an appetite for facilitation skills training in this growing community. Waterlution would begin to build the Waterlution "associate" role, responsible for organizing and facilitating workshops with support from Kun. This was a strategic effort to build the organization, while also offering skills training to emerging water leaders. One associate commented on this opportunity, "Waterlution has provided a safe and forgiving space for me to develop my facilitation skills. Together, these tools have empowered me as a water leader."

As Waterlution grew in both deliverables and staff, they were able to take more risks, and seek out more inspiration on how to create the amazing. Many different elements have been introduced over time, but two stand out. The first evolved from their thinking on play and creativity. Water theatre was introduced into the Waterlution programming, with an aim of blending entertainment with storytelling around water. This approach played to several principles of Waterlution's work. Storytelling connects us in ways that formal lectures cannot, it plays to our most human side of emotions, and engages us in a collective experience. A story can both remove us from reality, while at the same time be embedded in truth, which is perhaps why it is so powerful. Kun also continued to read widely and drew inspiration from many sources. A second important idea came from a Harvard Business Review article *To Drive Creativity, Add Some Conformity* (Miron-Spektor et al. 2012), who share that to build opportunities for innovation to emerge in team work, it is not enough to work with creative people, but that a collection of distinct cognitive types will lead to radical ideas. They suggest creatives should comprise 20-30% of the team, detail oriented individuals about 10%, and 10-20% should be conformists, with the remainder being more general thinkers. This focus on a specific mix of skills and capacity suggested there was more to think about than just getting a range of stakeholders to the conversation.

With considerable feedback, and learning over the first several years of Waterlution, it was time for more experimentation. Two new programs emerged. The first was the Canadian Water Innovation Lab held in Alberta in October 2010. Momentum was building for an event larger than the workshops with past participants being exposed to water ideas from across the country and wanting an opportunity to be in the same space together, to have first hand, dialogue and action on national water issues. 250 young Canadians, plus 50 newly trained Waterlution Facilitators attended a week-long Lab on water. The Lab, held at YMCA Camp Chief Hector near Canmore, was dubbed the "unconference for uncommon young leaders." The Lab incorporated resource guests, field trips, water theatre and sleepovers (some in teepees), but perhaps the most innovative part was that core elements of the Lab were to be designed by those who attended. Waterlution would be one of the first in Canada to apply the unconference format, framed largely around open space technology where the focus of dialogue emerges from the participants present. Participants commented that two of the most important takeaways from the Lab were the creation of a mutually-supportive community of water actors and that they were inspired to make change in their own water worlds.

The second program was the Hubs that grew as a response to the feedback from the Lab. Participants shared that they wanted to stay connected to others doing water work, and to learn, but often it was the feelings of inspiration that seems most valuable to those attending. Alongside of this, participants attending Waterlution events were finding that getting pushed out of their comfort zones was providing them space and drive to innovate, to challenge, and most significantly breakout of the constraints they faced in their problem domains or areas of work. The Hubs were built as a causal, social and creatively safe space where all of these things could occur, and in doing so, further support capacity building amongst those who engaged. Hub events took place in several cities across Canada, where there was an expressed interest. As part of building the community, the Hubs are open to all and strive to engage those outside of water as well. The events would maintain some of the roots of Waterlution – resource guests, facilitated dialogue (from trained Hub Managers) and a comfortable environment. Perhaps more importantly, is what the Hubs did not include; panel discussions and Q&A's. Kun strongly believes that the traditional conference set-up of one-way dialogue must evolve into facilitated dialogue. Instead, mentors or resource guests would be invited to share their experience by responding to questions such as, "what do you think is important for change makers to know?" One specific design principle was to allow the format of the Hubs to emerge and respond to the feedback that was received. Planning for Hubs became grounded by asking "how can we bring in the arts community to communicate about water in new and different ways?" The Hubs evolved to include element of the arts and provocateurs to push the comfort boundaries and engage the "amazing" such as composing music for the hydrolophone and choreographing a contemporary dance to match. A second intention of the Hubs was to continue to offer opportunities for individuals to build their own facilitation capacity. As the Hub events grew with interest, participants were invited to stretch their own facilitation and design legs, and they could become co-creators of the events with Waterlution.

Waterlution's Impact

With the 10-year anniversary of the organization just recently past, Kun has continued to think about how to measure Waterlution's impact, and work is underway to craft insightful measures for this unique organization. Ahead of this project, several associates and participants shared some of their perspectives on how they have seen Waterlution impact water work in Canada. They shared that, Waterlution has influenced how young leaders operate within the water sector, "it empowers the next generation of decision makers to think differently about how we do our jobs, make decisions, influence the agenda." It has opened doors about how to work through deep-seated challenges, "Waterlution has also demonstrated how to truly work across sectors and move beyond the nemesis of 'them' which is really critical to generating intelligent responses to the challenges that we face." It has introduced diverse inputs into the decision making process, "as an organization I think Waterlution has played an incredibly important role in breaking water policy and water management out of the 'science without humanity' mold that was a basis for many decisions and programs." Finally, Waterlution encouraged participants to try, fail, and try again, "Waterlution nudged me to think and act outside my comfort zone. Try it, test it. See what works, and what doesn't. That's good advice to solve water challenges, but also for life."

Lessons from Waterlution

Often when we want to begin a new project or start an organization, the first thing we do is ask, "how have others done this?" The story of Waterlution offers many valuable insights for starting and building a creative organization that is both stable and nimble. Waterlution was grounded by the kind of organization it wanted to be, one based on the chaordic principle – engaging both chaos and order. Returning regularly to this principle helped the organization to decide how, when and where to grow.

This principle also signals another important trait of the organization – that the co-founders were often looking externally for inspiration, new ideas, and concepts that would challenge, but ultimately grow their work. They made a concerted effort to be exposed to new ideas, to make themselves uncomfortable and then combine all that learning with what they already knew to create and transform opportunities for the organization.

Waterlution also lives and breathes prototyping – test, revise, test, revise. This fosters an environment of experimentation and limit testing, while simultaneously generating a safe space to play. Importantly, this is linked to the leadership style found in Kun, who asks, "can Waterlution exist in the world without it being connected to me?" She intentionally seeks to create space, and to enable the capacity for other leaders to emerge within the broader water world by providing learning opportunities to help get them there, and building a connected network that supports each other. But this also happens within her own organization, as "associates" host Waterlution workshops, or for the Hub manager to drive the Hub events with her own design intentions.

Waterlution's stability as an organization has much to do with the foundation that was laid in the early days. Kun, as the face of the organization recognized the need to build her own credibility within the water world, and invested the time to show up and build her network, and to learn from the experts in the field. This permitted her to operate from a place of deep knowledge, while also building a community of practitioners that were interested in the work. Often these were young professionals, who were stretching and growing in their own career alongside Waterlution stretching and growing as an organization – there was a mutually supportive relationship between the two, and each became invested in the other. Kun references an article by Margaret Wheatley and Debroah Frieze, *Using Emergence to take Social Innovation to Scale*, that discusses the value and impact of networks,

"The world doesn't change one person at a time. It changes as networks of relationships form among people who discover they share a common cause and vision of what's possible… We need to connect with kindred spirits. Through these relationships, we will develop the knowledge, practices, courage and commitment that lead to broad-based change." (Wheatley and Frieze 2006)

This notion of networks and mutually supported learning were always a part of the core tenants of Waterlution. One participant shared that the learning and connecting come back to them often in their own work, "the connections and takeaway messages seem to "pop up" in unexpected ways over time. That's the real magic of Waterlution's network. It's a long-term strategy." While another noted the compadre spirit between those in the Waterlution community, "It's been really inspiring to meet with the distributed network of individuals that seem to rally each time they find out about an interesting new activity going on in the Waterlution world." A final comment from a participant captures an additional element of the network, the collective knowledge that is being built, "Waterlution has created a community, in the truest sense of the word. While it exists both in-person at events, it also exists online across geographies, where often people don't meet each other but support and encourage the work of their water colleagues, and build our collective 'water brain' by sharing what is happening across the country on water and where people can contribute." Waterlution's purpose is to "inspire pattern-making and pattern-breaking change towards a healthy and sustainable relationship with water." The network is the result of the events, where people have been able to build a community, develop skills, and shift their thinking on how to approach water problems. The network, the people and their capacity that populate it, is the long-term strategy.

References

Bateson, P., and Martin, P. 2013. *Play, Playfulness, Creativity and Innovation*. New York, NY: Cambridge University Press.

Hock, D. 1999. *Birth of the Chaordic Age*. San Francisco, CA: Berrett-Koehler Publishers Inc.

Miron-Spektor, E., Erez, M., and Naveh, E. 2012. To Drive Creativity, Add Some Conformity. *Harvard Business Review*. http://hbr.org/2012/03/to-drive-creativity-add-some-conformity/ar/pr.

Nassbaum, N. 2013. *Creative Intelligence: Harnessing the Power to Create, Connect and Inspire*. New York, NY: Harper Business.

Wheatley, M., and Frieze, D. 2006. *Using Emergence to Take Social Innovations to Scale*. The Berkana Institute, http://berkana.org/berkana_articles/lifecycle-of-emergence-using-emergence-to-take-social-innovation-to-scale/.

Conclusion

Seanna Davidson, Ph.D.
Research Fellow, Systemic Governance Research Program, Monash University, Australia

Suzanne von der Porten, Ph.D.
Post-Doctoral Fellow, Hakai Network for Coastal People, Ecosystems and Management, Simon Fraser University

Those of us working in the water community could probably rattle off the laundry list of water challenges Canada faces without blinking, we're hit over the head with them everywhere we turn: urban runoff and sewage, agriculture, and industrial activities, population growth, economic development, climate change, and scarce fresh water supplies (CESD 2010). We see and experience these problems day in and day out. We are frustrated by the governance fragmentation in our workplaces where at least 20 federal agencies have responsibilities regarding water management, covered under 11 different pieces of federal legislation (NRTEE 2010). We can't access the scientific data we need from governments, and increasingly, it does not exist due to lack of funding (Gibbins and Sommerfeld 2011). We are caught in the middle of wanting a healthy growing economy, but know how thirsty our natural resource sector is. While this sector brings in approximately 12.5% of the country's GDP, it also consumes 84% of the total water withdrawn from our watersheds (NRTEE 2010). We miss swimming in our favorite waters because of eutrophication, where for Lake Winnipeg this means being named the most threatened Lake in the world (Global Nature Fund 2013). We're racked by the estimated \$80-\$90 billion price tag to upgrade Canada's water infrastructure (Watanabe 2010). We are aggravated by the loss of safe, drinkable, water due to leaky and deteriorating infrastructure, where in Montreal this accounts up to 40% of the supply (Watanabe 2010). We feel despair at the unconscionable numbers in First Nation communities where over 100 of those communities are currently under unsafe drinking water advisories, some for as long as 10 years (RBC Blue Water Project 2013) and where 39% of on-reserve water systems were classified "high overall risk" (Neegan Burnside 2011). We fight against the dismantling of our most precious piece of water legislation; *Canadian Environmental Assessment Act, Fisheries Act, Navigable Waters Protection Act* (Wilson 2013). We become disillusioned when we hear that 26% of Ontarians feel it is not their responsibility to protect drinking water, that three-quarters of Canadians use the toilet as a garbage can (RBC Blue Water Project 2014), and that people will pay more for cable, than they will for water (Gibbins and Sommerfeld 2011).

Then we ask ourselves, why doesn't anyone else care? Taken together, look at the words we're using to describe our relationship with water…frustrated, caught, missed, unconscionable, racked, despair, fight, disillusioned. We've hit the wall enough to know that we need to do things differently, and what we're beginning to uncover is that doing things differently with water suggests a host of opportunities that go beyond water itself, and hang most critically on the social dynamics of humans and their interactions with water.

In the preceding chapters, our contributors have provided examples of social opportunities for how we engage with our water. This contrasts with the "crisis" view of water management, and transcends the limitations of water as simply a business or economic opportunity. The chapters of this book have outlined the innovative – and positive – way in which people in Canada and beyond are turning water challenges into opportunities that benefit not only their own communities but society more broadly. The innovations are embedded in practices that range from collaboration and participatory democracy, to leadership and policy-making. Like previous eras shaped by how they respond to great water challenges (Solomon et al. 2011), so too is Canada's water landscape being shaped by these innovations underway.

The first section of the book contextualizes water problems in Canada looking at the macro scale of turning them into social opportunity. In the case of the drinking water crisis in First Nations communities in Canada, Phare and Mulligan point out that solutions go beyond the technical and the legal. Technologies for clean water distribution have been known for centuries. The opportunity with First Nations drinking water is the "process of collective decolonization to take root among non-Indigenous Canadians as well as among Indigenous people in Canada." Pentland also discusses crisis scenarios for Canada, as well as social opportunities for water and the environment more broadly. Policy-making and governance in Canada should aim for this best-case scenario in which Canada takes a "leadership role in the alternative energy and environmental fields." Schmidt reiterates that the demands on Canada's water systems are complex in nature. However, his suggestion is that the very narrative that links science to policy, can be reimagined, thus creating policy options for positions and values related to water.

The second section of this book furthers our understanding of water as a social opportunity through the introduction of emerging and potential innovative structures for policy development. One example is re-examining the assumptions we make surrounding the realms of the human and the non-human in the context of governance for water. Cohen argues that rather than making decisions at human-constructed political-scales or jurisdictions, decisions and policies should be and are increasingly made at a watershed scale. The example of municipal water supply governance in Ontario gives us yet another opportunity to rethink our approach to alternative and innovative governance for water (Furlong this book). In the Albertan context, Bjornland and Bjornland describe the opportunities being utilized by stakeholders for greater public participation in water planning directly with the Minister of Environment.

The third section is dedicated to inspiring transformative politics and innovative processes in Canada. The countrywide and ever-growing effect of organizations such as *Waterlution* that constantly innovate to connect people to each other and to water are described by Davidson. Similarly, Findlay demonstrates how processes like roundtable discussions integrate more people and thus better ideas into watershed management approaches. Finally, Van Welter inspires us to put on our party hats, pull up our sleeves, and be a part of re-imagining a new future of water, by remembering that we, just as water, are a part of the same system, and the solutions we are seeking are embedded in this symbiotic relationship.

Rich in Innovation, Ingenuity and Opportunity

We are a county rich in ingenuity, and amid social-political barriers to protecting freshwater from diversion, depletion and pollution (Barlow 2007), social entrepreneurs from coast to coast to coast are finding opportunities to transcend them. Alongside some of the innovations described in this book, many other social opportunities for water have been emerging across the country. Indigenous peoples, governments, and watershed groups are building their own opportunities in order to make decisions about waters that are important to them.

Nobody has shown more ingenuity and innovation at seizing opportunities than Indigenous peoples in Canada. Indigenous peoples have been plagued by centuries of colonization, including usurpation of their traditional territories, the intergenerational trauma of residential schools, and in more recent times, the destruction and/or contamination of their lands and waters. Despite this, Indigenous peoples are continuing to make great strides to protect the lands that they have lived on for time immemorial, including the protection of their marine and freshwater environments. For example, the Council of the Haida Nation, the Heiltsuk Tribal Council and the Nuu-chah-nulth Tribal Council on the British Columbia Coast are finding ways to innovate using collaboration to protect their traditional herring spawn-on-kelp fishery (CHN 2014; NTC 2014). Similarly, Anishinawbe men and women have been exercising forms of decolonization by walking around the Great Lakes to raise awareness about the need for protecting those waters (Phare and Mulligan, this book). The leadership being taken by Indigenous peoples in Canada to overcome the ongoing threats to their waters provides a strong example of innovation for other leaders worldwide.

People in the Maritime Provinces are demonstrating a variety of actions being taken to turn challenges into opportunities. The St. John's River, which flows through New Brunswick, was so badly contaminated in the 1960s it was once considered "on its deathbed" (Merrill and Hendriks 2012). However, watershed groups have been coming together to foster dialogue to share knowledge between riparian communities and to make positive changes in the future (Merrill and Hendriks 2012). New Brunswick has a strong history of grassroots watershed governance (Plummer and Stacey 2000) that was demonstrated recently where volunteer watershed stewardship groups worked with the Province to implement the Waters Classification Regulation (van Tol Smit et al. 2015). In the coming years, the people in New Brunswick will be engaging in "collaborative action to restore and sustain the health of the St. John River" (WWF 2011).

Leadership in seizing opportunities related to watershed governance have been further exemplified in Canada's north. The vast McKenzie Basin, spanning three provinces and two territories, has inspired innovations in both governance and policy-making. The Northwest Territories' 2010 document *Northern Voices, Northern Waters: NWT Water Stewardship* Strategy (Northwest Territories 2010) was written to guide policy in managing the large portion of the Basin that lies within the NWT. However, being downstream of Alberta's bitumen extraction from the "tar sands," the ramifications of NWT water policies related to quality and quantity extend well beyond territorial borders. The NWT's success in bringing together Indigenous peoples, and territorial and federal governments to create the stewardship strategy serves as model for other provinces and territories in Canada (Baltutis and Shah 2012). But the strategy also has the potential to serve as an example to other countries where natural resource extraction, colonized peoples, and complex problems confound the way to the solutions for innovative watershed governance.

Looking beyond individual organizations and governments, important developments on water as a social opportunity have taken place through the work of a loose network of multi-sector actors. Individually and collectively these actors are creating space for the economic and innovation opportunity around water technologies to emerge in Canada. Some of the core actors include The Royal Bank, The Walter and Duncan Gordan Foundation and the Canadian Water Network who formed the Blue Economy Initiative (launched in 2011). The Initiative has been conducting, and publishing research that builds the business case for water through identifying water's value to the economy, benefits of water sustainability and the risks of failure to act on water sustainability. The Blue

Economy Initiative (BEI) is a good example of promoting action based on the premise that water presents a broad range of social opportunities. Water Canada Magazine (originally Canadian Water Technology magazine, and launched in 2007, becoming Water Canada in 2010) has been the media outlet for water technology, economics, and policy in Canada as well as media sponsor to the, now annual, Canadian Water Summit (beginning in 2010). The Summit is a gathering of investors, industry and water technology firms to collaborate on water sustainability in Canada. This dialogue has been taking place alongside of efforts by the Ontario government to emerge as a water technology innovator, who in 2010 introduced the Water Opportunities and Water Conservation Act to accelerate this area of economic development in the province. Taken together, the BEI, Water Canada, and the Summit, they represent a specific and directed shift to raise, what has been identified in the past, as an underappreciated economic opportunity on water, one based on innovation and technology, rather than water exports.

The chapters in this book, and the examples above demonstrated how water as a social opportunity means more than just thinking positively, it means recognizing the potential to make deep structural changes in social relations through the way we respond to water problems. In a set of roundtables held in western Canada, a participant shared how we can re-frame our approach, "talk about the opportunity, talk about how great it will be if you get it right. Talk about how beautiful it will be, how prosperous it will be...We need to have this collective vision of how good it could be if we got this right" (Gibbins and Sommerfeld 2011). In that single statement, you can hear energy, positivity, and excitement even. What if we always started from this place? What could we come up with next that will further evolve our social dynamics with water? Or the perspective from which we choose to examine our water problems? Our institutions of decision-making, our processes for dialogue? We can see this thinking emerging with concepts like "water-energy nexus" (Watanabe 2010). We can hear the doors of opportunity open when we realize "the economic value of water's ecological services exceeds, by orders of magnitude, the value of industrial alternatives" (Renzetti et al. 2011). We can realize these opportunities when we implement whole system (ecosystem and society) plans, such as those imagined for Newfoundland and New Brunswick by the Council of Canadian Ministers of the Environment. They examined the pros and cons of upgrading all the sewage treatment plants in the two provinces and found that economic benefits from improved health, more productive ecosystems and attractive scenery over the 25-year life of the upgrades would exceed their cost by $204 million in Newfoundland and $450 million in New Brunswick (Sawyer et al. 2007). This is what social opportunity looks like, because it re-frames our relationship with water, as an individual, a community, and a country.

References

Baltutis, J., and Shah, T. 2012. *Cross-Canada Checkup: A Canadian Perspective on Our Water Future*. Victoria, BC: POLIS Project on Ecological Governance, University of Victoria. Available from http://poliswaterproject.org/publication/452.

Barlow, M. 2007. *Blue Covenant: The Global Water Crisis and the Coming Battle for the Right to Water*. New York, NY: New Press.

Commissionner of the Environment and Sustainable Development. 2010. *Fall Report of the Commissionner of the Environment and Sustainable Development*. Ottawa, ON: Government of Canada.

Council of the Haida Nation. February 4 2014. *An Open Letter to BC Commercial Herring Fishermen*. http://www.haidanation.ca/Pages/splash/public_notices/pdfs/CHN%20Herring%20Notice.pdf.

Gibbins, R., and Sommerfeld, L. 2011. *Wave of the Future: Water Policy in Western Canada*. Calgary, AB: Canada West Foundation.

Global Nature Fund. 2013. *Threatened Lake of the Year 2013: Lake Winnipeg in Canada*. Global Nature Fund, http://www.globalnature.org/35753/Living-Lakes/Threatened-Lake-2015/Threatened-Lake-2013/resindex.aspx.

Merrill, S., and Hendriks, E. 2012. *Making Connections on the St. John River: A River Tour Series Connecting the "State of the St. John" to Local Community Priorities for Actions on Our Rivers*: CCNB Action, Canadian Rivers Institute and WWF.

National Round Table on the Environment and Economy (NRTEE). 2010. *Changing Currents: Water Sustainability and the Future of Canada's Natural Resource Sectors*. Ottawa, ON: National Round Table on the Environment and Economy.

Neegan Burnside Ltd. 2011. *National Assessment of First Nations Water and Wastewater Systems: National Roll-up Report*. [Report prepared for the Department of Indian and Northern Affairs, Canada].

Northwest Territories. 2010. *Northern Voices, Northern Waters: Nwt Water Stewardship Strategy*: Northwest Territories, Canada.

Nuu-chah-nulth Tribal Council. January 31 2014. *An Open Letter to Bc Commercial Herring Fishermen*. http://www.hashilthsa.com/sites/default/files/Open%20letter%20to%20BC%20Herring%20Fishermen.pdf.

Plummer, R., and Stacey, C. 2000. A Multiple Case Study of Community-Based Water Management Initiatives in New Brunswick. *Canadian Water Resources Journal* 25(3): 293-307.

Renzetti, S., Dupont, D. P., and C.Wood. 2011. *Running through Our Fingers: How Canada Fails to Capture the Value of Its Top Asset*. Toronto, ON: Blue Economy Initiative.

Royal Bank of Canada Blue Water Project. 2013. *Ripple Effect: A Five-Year Report 2007-2012*. Toronto, ON: Royal Bank of Canada.

Royal Bank of Canada Blue Water Project. 2014. *Fluid Attitudes: Expert Opinions on the Findings of the 2014 RBC Canadian Water Attitudes Study*. Toronto, ON: Royal Bank of Canada.

Sawyer, D., Chung, L., and Renzetti, S. 2007. *Cost-Benefit Analysis for Cleaner Source Water*. [Report prepared for the Canadian Council of Ministers of the Environment] Ottawa, ON: Canadian Council of Ministers of the Environment.

Solomon, J., Jacobson, S. K., and Liu, I. 2011. Fishing for a Solution: Can Collaborative Resource Management Reduce Poverty and Support Conservation? *Environmental Conservation* 39(1): 51-61.

Van Tol Smit, E., Loë, R. d., and Plummer, R. 2015. How Knowledge Is Used in Collaborative Environmental Governance: Water Classification in New Brunswick, Canada. *Journal of Environmental Planning and Management* 48(3): 423-44.

Watanabe, A. M. 2010. *Water and the Future of the Canadian Economy*. Toronto, ON: The Innovolve Group.

Wilson, P. 2013. *The Blue Paper: Water Co-Governance in Canada*: Forum for Leadership on Water.

World Wildlife Fund (WWF) Canada. 2011. *The St. John River*. WWF Canada, http://www.wwf.ca/conservation/freshwater/the_st_john_river/.

Queen's Policy Studies
Recent Publications

The Queen's Policy Studies Series is dedicated to the exploration of major public policy issues that confront governments and society in Canada and other nations.

Manuscript submission. We are pleased to consider new book proposals and manuscripts. Preliminary inquiries are welcome. A subvention is normally required for the publication of an academic book. Please direct questions or proposals to the Publications Unit by email at spspress@queensu.ca, or visit our website at: www.queensu.ca/sps/books, or contact us by phone at (613) 533-2192.

Our books are available from good bookstores everywhere, including the Queen's University bookstore (http://www.campusbookstore.com/). McGill-Queen's University Press is the exclusive world representative and distributor of books in the series. A full catalogue and ordering information may be found on their web site (**http://mqup.mcgill.ca/**).

For more information about new and backlist titles from Queen's Policy Studies, visit http://www.queensu.ca/sps/books.

School of Policy Studies

Toward a Healthcare Strategy for Canadians, A. Scott Carson, Jeffrey Dixon, and Kim Richard Nossal (eds.) 2015. ISBN 978-1-55339-439-6

Work in a Warming World, Carla Lipsig-Mummé and Stephen McBride (eds.) 2015. ISBN 978-1-55339-432-7

Lord Beaconsfield and Sir John A. Macdonald: A Political and Personal Parallel, Michel W. Pharand (ed.) 2015. ISBN 978-1-55339-438-9

Canadian Public-Sector Financial Management, Second Edition, Andrew Graham 2014. ISBN 978-1-55339-426-6

The Multiculturalism Question: Debating Identity in 21st-Century Canada, Jack Jedwab (ed.) 2014. ISBN 978-1-55339-422-8

Government-Nonprofit Relations in Times of Recession, Rachel Laforest (ed.) 2013. ISBN 978-1-55339-327-6

Intellectual Disabilities and *Dual Diagnosis: An Interprofessional Clinical Guide for Healthcare Providers*, Bruce D. McCreary and Jessica Jones (eds.) 2013. ISBN 978-1-55339-331-3

Rethinking Higher Education: Participation, Research, and Differentiation, George Fallis 2013. ISBN 978-1-55339-333-7

Making Policy in Turbulent Times: Challenges and Prospects for Higher Education, Paul Axelrod, Roopa Desai Trilokekar, Theresa Shanahan, and Richard Wellen (eds.) 2013. ISBN 978-1-55339-332-0

Building More Effective Labour-Management Relationships, Richard P. Chaykowski and Robert S. Hickey (eds.) 2013. ISBN 978-1-55339-306-1

Navigationg on the Titanic: Economic Growth, Energy, and the Failure of Governance, Bryne Purchase 2013. ISBN 978-1-55339-330-6

Measuring the Value of a Postsecondary Education, Ken Norrie and Mary Catharine Lennon (eds.) 2013. ISBN 978-1-55339-325-2

Immigration, Integration, and Inclusion in Ontario Cities, Caroline Andrew, John Biles, Meyer Burstein, Victoria M. Esses, and Erin Tolley (eds.) 2012. ISBN 978-1-55339-292-7

Diverse Nations, Diverse Responses: Approaches to Social Cohesion in Immigrant Societies, Paul Spoonley and Erin Tolley (eds.) 2012. ISBN 978-1-55339-309-2

Making EI Work: Research from the Mowat Centre Employment Insurance Task Force, Keith Banting and Jon Medow (eds.) 2012. ISBN 978-1-55339-323-8

Managing Immigration and Diversity in Canada: A Transatlantic Dialogue in the New Age of Migration, Dan Rodríguez-García (ed.) 2012. ISBN 978-1-55339-289-7

International Perspectives: Integration and Inclusion, James Frideres and John Biles (eds.) 2012. ISBN 978-1-55339-317-7

Dynamic Negotiations: Teacher Labour Relations in Canadian Elementary and Secondary Education, Sara Slinn and Arthur Sweetman (eds.) 2012. ISBN 978-1-55339-304-7

Where to from Here? Keeping Medicare Sustainable, Stephen Duckett 2012. ISBN 978-1-55339-318-4

International Migration in Uncertain Times, John Nieuwenhuysen, Howard Duncan, and Stine Neerup (eds.) 2012. ISBN 978-1-55339-308-5

Centre for International and Defence Policy

Afghanistan in the Balance: Counterinsurgency, Comprehensive Approach, and Political Order, Hans-Georg Ehrhart, Sven Bernhard Gareis, and Charles Pentland (eds.), 2012. ISBN 978-1-55339-353-5

Institute of Intergovernmental Relations

Canada: The State of the Federation 2012, Loleen Berdahl, André Juneau, and Carolyn Hughes Tuohy (eds.), 2015. ISBN 978-1-55339-210-1

Canada: The State of the Federation 2011, Nadia Verrelli (ed.), 2014. ISBN 978-1-55339-207-1

Canada and the Crown: Essays on Constitutional Monarchy, D. Michael Jackson and Philippe Lagassé (eds.), 2013. ISBN 978-1-55339-204-0

Paradigm Freeze: Why It Is So Hard to Reform Health-Care Policy in Canada, Harvey Lazar, John N. Lavis, Pierre-Gerlier Forest, and John Church (eds.), 2013. ISBN 978-1-55339-324-5

Canada: The State of the Federation 2010, Matthew Mendelsohn, Joshua Hjartarson, and James Pearce (eds.), 2013. ISBN 978-1-55339-200-2

The Democratic Dilemma: Reforming Canada's Supreme Court, Nadia Verrelli (ed.), 2013. ISBN 978-1-55339-203-3